# ZOOM IN ...

## The Horrors of Utopia

Herausgegeben von:
Iris Faßbender und Colette Granvillano

Erarbeitet von:
Colette Granvillano und Alexander Krüger

Schöningh
westermann

Muttersprachliche Betreuung: Ronnie Halligan

westermann GRUPPE



Druck A[3] / Jahr 2018
Alle Drucke der Serie A sind im Unterricht parallel verwendbar.

Umschlaggestaltung: Reinhild Kassing, Kassel
Umschlagabbildung: © everlite/iStockphoto
Druck und Bindung: Westermann Druck GmbH, Braunschweig

ISBN 978-3-14-**040654**-3

# Zur Arbeit mit dem Buch

## Anforderungsbereiche

Alle Aufgaben dieses Bandes sind farbig gekennzeichnet und sind somit den drei Anforderungsbereichen eindeutig zuzuordnen. Eine detaillierte Aufstellung aller Operatoren finden Sie im Anhang.

AFB I: Comprehension

AFB II: Analysis

AFB III: Evaluation/Re-creation of text

Aufgaben, die einen Text inhaltlich/sprachlich vorbereiten beziehungsweise weiterführend vertiefen, sind grau unterlegt.

## Symbole

Auf verschiedenen Seiten dieses Bandes finden Sie Symbole, die auf sprachlich-methodische Fertigkeiten, Musterlösungen und weiterführende Aktivitäten hinweisen.

*Speaking* – Mithilfe dieser Aufgabe wird der mündliche Ausdruck geübt.

*Listening* – Zu diesem Material gibt es im Lehrerband eine Audio-Datei (auf CD), mit der das Hörverstehen geschult wird.

*Mediation* – Dieses Material wird in eigenen Worten auf Englisch wiedergegeben und dient der Sprachmittlung.

*Model solution* – Zu dieser Aufgabe liegt eine Musterlösung vor.

*Activity* – Bei dieser Aufgabe werden die Schülerinnen und Schüler in vielfältiger Weise selbst aktiv.

## Webcodes

Webcodes verweisen auf Zusatzmaterial im Internet und erleichtern Ihnen das Auffinden von Links und Dateien, die speziell für den vorliegenden Band ausgewählt oder erstellt wurden.

@ SNG-40654-001

Zur Nutzung gehen Sie bitte auf folgende Seite: http://www.schoeningh-schulbuch.de/webcodes

Geben Sie dort den Code ein, um zu dem jeweiligen Material zu gelangen.

# Contents

# Getting started

> A map of the world that does not include UTOPIA is not worth even glancing at, for it leaves out the one country at which humanity is always landing.
>
> OSCAR WILDE

| 1895 | 1932 | 1945 | 1949 | 1953 | 1954 | 1962 |
|---|---|---|---|---|---|---|
| H.G. Wells *The Time Machine* | Aldous Huxley *Brave New World* | George Orwell *Animal Farm* | George Orwell *1984* | Ray Bradbury *Fahrenheit 451* | William Golding *Lord of the Flies* | Anthony Burgess *A Clockwork Orange* |

With reference to the quote and the picture provided, design your personal future society. Consider the following questions:

- What kind of political system should your society have?
- What role should culture and religion play in your society?
- In what ways, if at all, would you try to influence the reproduction of your people? How should your children be brought up and educated?
- How would you deal with progress in technology, medicine etc.?

Present your findings on a poster or on a transparency in class.

| 1982 | 1985 | 1992 | 2002 | 2004 | 2008 | 2013 |
|---|---|---|---|---|---|---|
| Richard Bachman (aka Stephen King) *The Running Man* | Margaret Atwood *The Handmaid's Tale* | P.D. James *The Children of Men* | M.T. Anderson *Feed* | David Mitchell *Cloud Atlas* | Suzanne Collins *The Hunger Games* | Dave Eggers *The Circle* |

# Visions of the Future

## M 1 The Horrors of Utopia

Stephen Duncombe

The following abstract is taken from the introductory notes of *Open Utopia*, a free, online version of Thomas More's *Utopia* that everyone can browse and annotate. This project can be called social reading, based on the idea that a book does not have to be a static text. It serves as a meeting place for readers to exchange their opinions and reactions to the book. In his introduction to *Open Utopia* Stephen Duncombe defines the concept of Utopia and elaborates on its relevance for society.

1. Explain the saying "one man's utopia is another man's dystopia".
2. **State** why "we need Utopia" (l. 10) and **point out** why "Utopia can [...] be problematic" (l. 40).
3. **Examine** the role of "criticism" as presented in the text.
4. **Assess** whether or not "criticism" is the antithesis of utopia.
5. **Evaluate** the role of criticism in the context of your perfect world. Should e. g. political criticism be included in your perfect society?

Utopia is a hard sell in the twenty-first century. Today we are people who know better, and what we know are the horrors of "actually existing" Utopias of the previous century: Nazi Germany, Stalin's Soviet Union, Maoist China, and so on in depressing repetition. In each case there was a radical break with the present and a bold leap toward an imagined future; in every case the result was disastrous in terms of human cost. Thankfully, what seems to be equally consistent is that these Utopias were relatively short-lived. History, therefore, appears to prove two things: one, Utopias, once politically realized, are staggering* in their brutality; and two, they are destined* to fail. Not exactly a ringing endorsement*.

Yet we need Utopia more than ever. We live in a time without alternatives, at "the end of history" as Francis Fukuyama would have it, when neoliberal capitalism reins triumphant and uncontested*. There are still aberrations*: radical Islam in the East, neo-fascist xenophobia in the West, and a smattering* of socialist societies struggling around the globe, but by and large the only game in town is the global free market. In itself this might not be so bad, except for the increasingly obvious fact that the system is not working, not for most people and not most of the time. Income inequality has increased dramatically both between and within nations. National autonomy has become subservient* to the imperatives of global economic institutions, and federal, state, and local governance are undermined by the protected power of money. Profit-driven industrialization and the headlong

**staggering** astounding
**destined** certain to happen
**endorsement** strong support
**uncontested** not challenged, not called into question
**aberration** different view from the norm
**smattering** small amount
**subservient** obedient, submissive

rush toward universal consumerism is hastening the ecological destruction of the planet. In short: the world is a mess. Opinion polls, street protests, and volatile* voting patterns demonstrate widespread dissatisfaction with the current system, but the popular response so far has largely been limited to the angry outcry of *No!* No to dictators, No to corruption, No to finance capital, No to the one percent who control everything. But negation, by itself, affects nothing. The dominant system dominates not because people agree with it; it rules because we are convinced there is no alternative.

Utopia offers us a glimpse of an alternative. Utopia, broadly conceived, is an image of a world not yet in existence that is different from and better than the world we inhabit now. For the revolutionary, Utopia offers a goal to reach and a vision to be realized. For the reformer, it provides a compass point to determine what direction to move toward and a measuring stick to determine how far one has come. Utopia is politically necessary even for those who do not desire an alternative society at all. Thoughtful politics depend upon debate and without someone or something to disagree with there is no meaningful dialogue, only an echo chamber. Utopia offers this "other," an interlocutor* with which to argue, thereby clarifying and strengthening your own ideas and ideals (even if they lead to the conclusion that Utopia is undesirable). Without a vision of an alternative future, we can only look backwards nostalgically to the past, or unthinkingly maintain what we have, mired* in the unholy apocalypse that is now. Politically, we need Utopia. [...]

Between the two poles of the political spectrum, for those in the center who simply hold on to the ideal of democracy, Utopia can also be problematic. Democracy is a system in which ordinary people determine, directly or through representation, the system that governs the society they live within. Utopias, however, are usually the products of singular imaginations or, at best, the plans of a small group: a political vanguard* or artistic avant-garde. Utopians too often consider people as organic material to be shaped, not as willful agents who do the shaping; the role of the populace* is, at best, to conform to a plan of a world already delivered complete. Considered a different way, Utopia is a closed program in which action is circumscribed* by an algorithm coded by the master programmer. In this program there is no space for the citizen hacker. This is one reason why large-scale Utopias, made manifest, are so horrific and short-lived: short-lived because people tend not to be so pliable*, and therefore insist on upsetting the perfect plans for living; horrific because people are made pliable and forced to fit the plans made for them. In Utopia the *demos** is designed, not consulted. It is precisely the imaginative quality of Utopia – that is, the singular dream of a phantasmagorical* alternative – that seems to damn the project to naïve impracticality as an ideal and megalomaniac* brutality in its realization. But without political illusions, with what are we left? Disillusion, and its attendant discursive* practice: criticism. Earnest, ironic, sly or bombastic; analytic, artistic, textual, or performative; criticism has become *the* predominant political practice of intellectuals, artists, and even activists who are dissatisfied with the world of the present, and ostensibly* desire something new. Criticism is also Utopia's antithesis. If Utopianism is the act of imagining what is new, criticism, derived from the Greek words *kritikos* (to judge) and perhaps more revealing, *krinein* (to separate or divide), is the practice of pulling apart, examining, and judging that which already exists.

Stephen Duncombe, "Open Utopia", in: Thomas More, Open | Utopia, ed. by Stephen Duncombe, Minor Compositions, Wivenhoe/New York/Port Watson 2012, p. IX ff., http://theopenutopia.org


**volatile** unpredictable

**interlocutor** dialogue partner

**to be mired in** to be stuck in

**vanguard** leaders in the forefront of a movement

**populace** population

**to circumscribe** to define

**pliable** flexible, bendable, obedient

**demos** Greek for: citizen

**phantasmagorical** fantastic, visionary

**megalomaniac** the will to have power and control over other people

**discursive** gaining knowledge through reason rather than intuition

**ostensibly** apparently, evidently

## M2 Dystopian Books Again Seize Power

Dystopia is defined as "an imaginary place or state in which the condition of life is extremely bad, as from deprivation, oppression, or terror"[1]. Dystopian fiction is "the creation of a nightmare world, or dystopia"[2].

1. **Describe** the graph with the help of the vocabulary provided.

2. Now use your detailed description and try to **explain** why people tend to prefer dystopian fiction in troubled times.

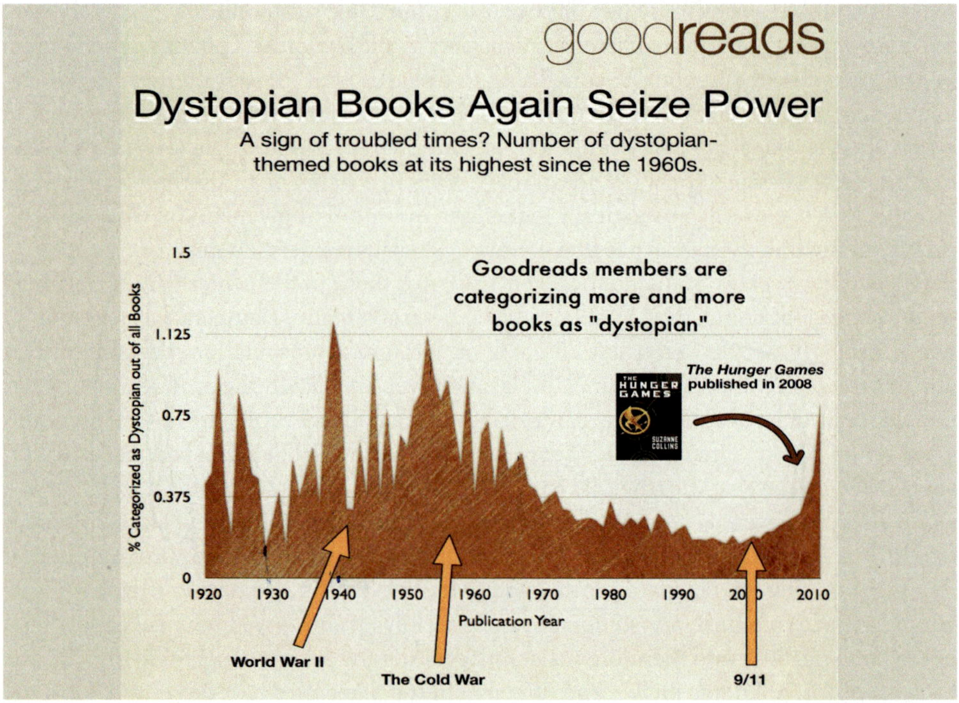


taken from: www.goodreads.com, 21.03.2012 [29.01.2014]

3. In the visual above, three landmarks in world history are already given (World War II, The Cold War and 9/11). Do further research on landmarks in world history using the given time frame and create a timeline in which you show the connection between dystopian fiction and crucial events in world history. For more dystopian literature consider the Getting started page (p. 6/7).

**Zoom in: Vocabulary**

**Analysing a line graph**

to reach a peak/a low point of ... • to remain constant/stable • to go through a period of growth/decline/stagnation • to increase/rise/decrease/fall by ... • gradual/steady/continuous growth/decline • sharp/noticeable/extreme growth/decline

---

[1] The American Heritage Dictionary of the English Language, Fourth Edition copyright © 2000 by Houghton Mifflin Company. Updated in 2009. Published by Houghton Mifflin Company.

[2] "Utopian and dystopian fiction", http://en.wikipedia.org [24.03.2014]

**ZOOM IN: Terminology**

Coloured illustration for the 1516 first edition of *Utopia*

The term **Utopia** was first coined by Sir Thomas More for his book *Utopia*, published back in 1516. The term has a double meaning, either "no place" or "good place" (both derived from Greek). A utopia describes a future imaginary society in which everything appears better than in our current world. This might involve science, technology and the political system, i. e. democracy and participation. Back in the 19th century, the technological process was seen as something positive and inspiring. Inventions such as, amongst other things, the steam engine and new medicines made people hope for a better future and possible dangers or threats were not considered at that time.

This attitude changed when the speed of progress increased. Not only the benefits but also the disadvantages and even the threats started to become obvious. One crucial event shaping people's minds about progress, science and technology was World War I with its highly developed new weaponry which led to millions of dead and injured. A more negative vision of the future emerged, fostered also by the experience of authoritarian, inhumane political regimes (Nazi Germany, the Soviet Union) and World War II which in turn can be seen or labelled as "anti-utopia" or **dystopia**. Here, the concept of extrapolation comes into play, meaning that contemporary technologies and scientific trends are thought one or several levels further and projected into an imaginary future. New technologies play a big role in dystopian fiction due to the fact that they have a crucial impact on the structure of society as a whole.

**Science fiction** is, however, a different literary genre. Here, the focus does not lie on society and human life but rather on the possibilities opened up by science and technology.

## M 3 Oryx and Crake

### Margaret Atwood

In *Oryx and Crake*, Margaret Atwood depicts a near-future world in which Snowman (a man once known as Jimmy) sleeps in a tree and might be the only human left on our devastated planet. He is not entirely alone, however, as he considers himself the shepherd of a group of experimental, human-like creatures called the Children of Crake. Snowman recalls in flashbacks how the world fell apart. Jimmy's best friend was "Crake," a brilliant science student. Crake gets Jimmy a job with a biotech corporation where Crake is designing the Crakers – a new, multi-coloured placid race of human beings, smelling vaguely of citron.
In this passage, Snowman/Jimmy – on his way to the compound of the biotech corporation – hears the mating Crakers and reflects on a conversation he once had with Crake.

**1.** **Describe** the mating process of the Crakers.

**2.** Choose either Crake or Jimmy (Snowman) and **examine** the view on mating and art held by the respective character by filling in the table accordingly. Give evidence from the text to prove your findings (cf. l. ?/ll. ??) Then find someone who has worked on the other character and exchange your results. Make notes on what your partner tells you.

| | Crake | Jimmy (snowman) |
|---|---|---|
| attitude towards mating and art | | |
| presentation of the character | | |

**3.** Would you tend to agree with Crake or with Jimmy? **Justify** your choice.

**quintuplet** five babies born to the same mother at the same time, here: a group of five
**to filch** to steal
**chromophore** the part of a molecule responsible for the colour of a compound
**whiff** a slight amount, smell or sign of sth.

**semaphore** *Flaggensignal*
**ardour** great enthusiasm or passion
**to dissipate** (as of a feeling) to disappear

**pimp** a man who earns money by finding customers for prostitutes
**to roister** to enjoy or celebrate in a noisy way
**vulva** the outer parts of a woman's sexual organs

**romp** an occasion on which people have sex without intending to have a serious relationship
**misalignment** the incorrect arrangement or position of sth. in relation to sth. else

[...] There must be a mating going on, a rare-enough occasion among the people: Crake had worked out the numbers, and had decreed that once every three years per female was more than enough.

There'll be the standard quintuplet*, four men and the woman in heat. Her condition will be obvious to all from the bright-blue colour of her buttocks and abdomen – a trick of variable pigmentation filched* from the baboons with a contribution from the expandable chromophores* of the octopus. [...]

Courtship begins at the first whiff*, the first faint blush of azure, with the males presenting flowers to the females – just as male penguins present round stones, said Crake, or as the male silverfish presents a sperm packet. At the same time they indulge in musical out-bursts, like songbirds. Their penises turn bright blue to match the blue abdomens of the females, and they do a sort of blue-dick dance number, erect members waving to and fro in unison, in time to the foot movements and the singing: a feature suggested to Crake by the sexual semaphoring* of crabs. From amongst the floral tributes the female chooses four flowers, and the sexual ardour* of the unsuccessful candidates dissipates* immediately, with no hard feelings left. Then, when the blue of her abdomen has reached its deepest shade, the female and her quartet find a secluded spot and go at it until the woman becomes pregnant and her blue colouring fades. And that is that.

No more *No means yes*, anyway, thinks Snowman. No more prostitution, no sexual abuse of children, no haggling over the price, no pimps*, no sex slaves. No more rape. The five of them will roister* for hours, three of the men standing guard and doing the singing and shouting while the fourth one copulates, turn and turn about. Crake has equipped these women with ultra-strong vulvas* – extra skin layers, extra muscles – so they can sustain these marathons. It no longer matters who the father of the inevitable child may be, since there's no more property to inherit, no father–son loyalty required for war. Sex is [...] like an athletic demonstration, a free-spirited romp*. [...]

"How much misery," Crake said one lunchtime – this must have been when they were in their early twenties and Crake was already at the Watson-Crick Institute – "how much needless despair has been caused by a series of biological mismatches, a misalignment* of the hormones and pheromones? Resulting in the fact that the one you love so passionately won't or can't love you. As a species we're pathetic in that way: imperfectly monogamous. If we could only pair-bond for life, like gibbons, or else opt for total guilt-free promiscuity, there'd be no more sexual torment. Better plan – make it cyclical and also inevitable, as in the other mammals. You'd never want someone you couldn't have."

"True enough," Jimmy replied. [...] "But think what we'd be giving up."

"Such as?"

"Courtship behaviour. In your plan we'd just be a bunch of hormone robots." [...] What he meant was the challenge, the excitement, the chase. "There'd be no free choice."

"There's courtship behaviour in my plan," said Crake, "except that it would always succeed. And we're hormone robots anyway, only we're faulty ones."

"Well, what about art?" said Jimmy [...].

"What about it?" said Crake, smiling his calm smile.

"All that mismatching you talk about. It's been an inspiration [...]. Think of all the poetry – think Petrarch*, think John Donne*, think the *Vita Nuova**, think ..."

"Art," said Crake. "[...] What is it Byron* said? Who'd write if they could do otherwise? [...]"

"That's what I mean," said Jimmy. [...] "I mean, when you can't get the *otherwise*, then ..."

"Wouldn't you rather be fucking?" said Crake. [...]

Jimmy found that his face got redder and his voice got squeakier the more outrageous Crake became. He hated that. "When any civilization is dust and ashes," he said, "art is all that's left over. Images, words, music. Imaginative structures. Meaning – human meaning, that is – is defined by them. You have to admit that."

"That's not quite all that's left over," said Crake. "The archaeologists are just as interested in gnawed bones and old bricks and ossified* shit these days. Sometimes more interested. They think human meaning is defined by those things too." [...]

"What have you got against it?" [...]

"Nothing," said Crake lazily. "People can amuse themselves any way they like. [...] Anyway it serves a biological purpose. [...] The male frog, in mating season [...] makes as much noise as it can. The females are attracted to the male frog with the biggest, deepest voice because it suggests a more powerful frog, one with superior genes. Small male frogs – it's been documented – discover that if they position themselves in empty drainpipes, the pipe acts as a voice amplifier, and the small frog appears much larger than it really is."

"So?"

"So that's what art is, for the artist," said Crake. "An empty drainpipe. An amplifier. A stab at getting laid." [...]

Margaret Atwood, *Oryx and Crake*, Anchor Books, New York 2003, p. 193–198



**Petrarch** (1304–74) Italian poet/sonneteer
**John Donne** (1572–1631) English poet and preacher
**Vita Nuova** verse and prose work by Dante Alighieri (1265–1321)
**Byron** (1788–1824) English poet

**to ossifiy** to turn into bone or bony tissue

## Zoom in: People

Margaret Atwood

The Canadian writer **Margaret Atwood**, born on 18 November 1939 in Ottawa, studied English and Literature at the University of Toronto and at Harvard University. She published her first novel, *The Edible Woman*, in 1969. Today, she is respected as Canada's most important novelist since her stories very often deal with the role of women in society but she also addresses current issues, such as ecological questions. She became famous for her novel *The Handmaid's Tale*, which was also made into a film. The story is set in the fictitious Republic of Gilead, where a group of conservative religious extremists has deprived women of their rights. Pollution and sexually transmitted diseases have created an ever more sterile society and thus women are intended to serve reproductive purposes only.

Atwood wrote this novel during a time when, after the "sexual revolution" of the 1960s and 1970s, more conservative values concerning the feminist movement started to spread in the West, accompanying the election of the Republican Ronald Reagan as US-president in 1981, and that of the "Iron Lady" Margaret Thatcher as British Prime Minister in 1979. Atwood won several awards for this novel.

# M 4 The Testament of Jessie Lamb

## Jane Rogers

The novel, published in 2011, centres around Jessie Lamb, a 16-year-old girl who wants to save humanity. The Maternal Death Syndrome, a virus affecting pregnant women, threatens the survival of mankind as a whole. Jesse decides to take part in a programme in which she will be injected with an immune embryo, but she also knows that she will not recover from the coma that will be necessary to enable the birth of her child. Since her parents strongly oppose her decision, they imprison her.
Rogers is well-known for her novel *Island* (2000) which has also been turned into a film in 2011. *The Testament of Jessie Lamb* was long-listed for the *Man Booker Prize for Fiction* in 2011 and won the *Arthur C. Clarke Award* in 2011.

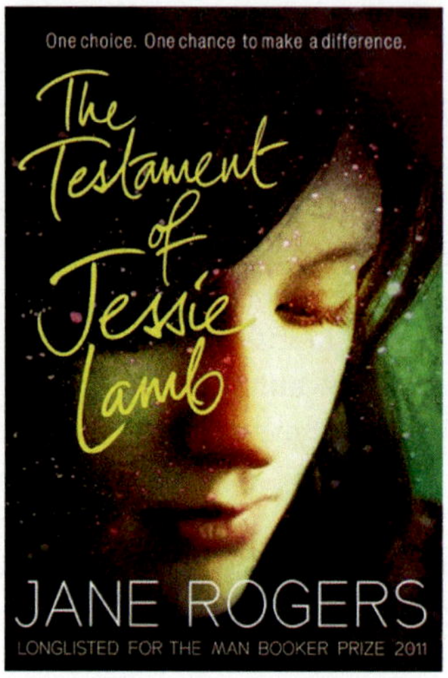


1. **Describe** the new disease mentioned in this excerpt, how and why it has come about, who it affects, and how it works.
2. **Analyse** the relationship between father and daughter as shown in this excerpt. Focus on the narrative perspective as well as the tone and style of their dialogue.
3. With reference to this excerpt, **discuss** possible reasons that terrorist groups might have for unleashing a fatal virus on the world.
4. "Women are dying in their millions. Some blame scientists, some see the hand of God, some see human arrogance reaping the punishment it deserves." **Comment** on this quote (from the back of the book cover).

There was a Tuesday when Dad properly explained Maternal Death Syndrome to me. The news was saying it was everywhere. Rumours about unaffected tribes deep in the Amazon rainforest or amongst the Inuit of the frozen north, all of them were untrue. It wasn't just the West, or the First World, or cities. There *were* some pregnant women left, but only ones who were far on in their pregnancies; women who must have got pregnant before MDS arrived. Once these women gave birth, it seemed there wouldn't be any more babies.
'I don't understand,' I said to Dad. 'Why is it only pregnant women who get it?'
'Well,' he said, settling down to peel some potatoes. 'Up till 100 years ago, pregnancy was the most dangerous experience in a woman's life, and the one the highest percentage were likely to die from.'
'Father of Wisdom,' I said, and rolled my eyes at him. That's what I call him when he goes off on one. But he didn't smile.
'D'you want to know or don't you?'
'I want to know.'
'Right then. There are all sorts of reasons why pregnancy is dangerous – obviously. The baby can come too early or too late; it may not present head first, the placenta may not come away properly, etc. But once you take away all the physical, *mechanical* things that

can go wrong – there's something else, which is even more disturbing ...: because they think it's what these guys have latched on to.'

'These guys?'

'The terrorists. Bio-terrorists, who've engineered this virus.'

'What is it?'

'Well you know what your immune system is?'

'Yes, it fights diseases.'

'Exactly. It knows what *you* are, and it attacks anything that is not *you*. Anything foreign in your system, it attacks, in order to defend you. Now spot the problem. When a woman gets pregnant, what's the problem?'

I sat and puzzled my brain. 'Is it the baby? Because the baby's a different person?'

'Nearly. What's the baby made of?'

'Doh*. Blood, bones – '

He shook his head at me. 'In the very beginning.'

'An egg.'

'And?'

'A sperm.'

'Thank you. Which comes from someone else. And for the baby to grow, that sperm needs to survive, and all the cells that grow from the union of the sperm and the egg need to survive. But the woman's immune system should attack it. Because it's a foreigner in her body.'

'OK.'

'But it doesn't. In most normal pregnancies, the woman's immune system does not attack the sperm or developing foetus. Her immune system takes a step back, in order to let the baby grow. And while the woman's not being defended against the sperm, she's also not being completely defended against various other nasties* that might want to invade her system.'

'And that's why she gets MDS?'

'So they think. The blip* in her immune system, which allows her to remain pregnant, seems to make her vulnerable to Maternal Death Syndrome. That's when it kicks in. It's a freakish chance – whoever worked it out is either a genius or very lucky.'

'So when they say it's full-blown* – '

'They mean it's triggered CJD*. Prion* disease. They've married the AIDS virus with CJD, that's what researchers reckon. So the AIDS gets a hold and makes the woman vulnerable to everything going, and the first thing that's going is CJD. For which we have no cure in sight – never have had, not back since the days of Mad Cow disease*.'

'A scientist must have done it.'

'Well it hasn't happened by accident.'

'But *why*?'

'Power? Religion? Your guess is as good as mine, Jessie.'

Jane Rogers, *The Testament of Jessie Lamb*, Sandstone Press Ltd, Dingwall 2011, pp. 12–14.

**doh** an exclamation showing that you are annoyed at yourself, often accompanied by a slap on your forehead

**nasties** (infml.) *Scheußlichkeiten*

**blip** a short pause or change

**full-blown** at a most advanced stage
**CJD** Creutzfeldt-Jakob disease, an incurable and invariably fatal brain disease
**prion** a very small piece of protein that is thought to cause some brain diseases such as BSE, Bovine Spongiform Encephalopathy (**Mad Cow disease**)

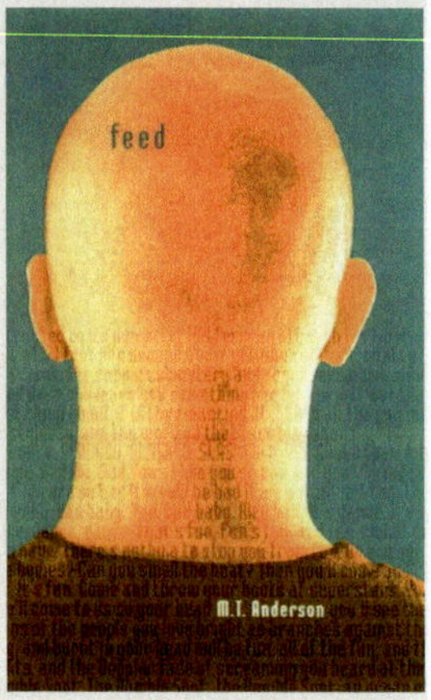


# M 5a Feed

M.T. Anderson

Anderson's novel *Feed* is set in the not-too-distant American future and depicts a society in which the Internet has developed into a 'Feednet' that everyone is connected to at birth through an implant into the brain. The novel deals with the relationship between the teenagers Titus and Violet. In **M 5a**, Titus is talking about the development of the 'feeds', in **M 5b**, Violet and Titus are chatting about society through their 'feeds'.

1. **Point out** how technological advances affect people's lives.
2. **Characterise** Titus's feelings concerning the 'feed'. Come up with suitable adjectives.
3. Find a partner who has worked on **Text B**. Exchange your results and **discuss** in how far you find the title of the novel appropriate.

I don't know when they first had feeds. Like maybe, fifty or a hundred years ago. Before that, they had to use their hands and their eyes. Computers were all outside the body. They carried them around outside of them, in their hands, like if you carried your lungs in a briefcase and opened it to breathe.

People were really excited when they first came out with feeds. It was all *da da da, this big educational thing, da da da, you child will have the advantage, encyclopedias at their fingertips, closer than their fingertips, etc.* That's one of the great things about the feed – that you can be supersmart without ever working. Everyone is supersmart now. You can look things up automatic, like science and history, like if you want to know which battles of the Civil War George Washington fought in and shit.

It's more now, it's not so much about the educational stuff but more regarding the fact that everything that goes on, goes on on the feed. All of the feedcasts and the instant news, that's on there, so there's all the entertainment I was missing without the feed, like the girls were all missing their favorite feedcast, this show call *Oh? Wow! Thing!*, which has all these kids like us who do stuff but get all pouty*, which is what the girls go crazy for, the poutiness.

But the braggest* thing about the feed, the thing that made it really big, is that it knows everything you want and hope for, sometimes before you even know what those things are. It can tell you how to get them, and help you make buying decisions that are hard. Everything we think and feel is taken in by the corporations, mainly by data ones like Feedlink and OnFeed and American Feedware, and they make a special profile, one that's keyed just to you, and then they give it to their branch companies, or other companies buy them, and they can get to know what it is we need, so all you have to do is want something and there's a chance it will be yours.

And it's really great to know everything about everything whenever we want, to have it just like, in our brain, just sitting there.

**to pout** *schmollen*

**brag** exceptionally fine

M.T. Anderson, *Feed*, Candlewick Press, Somerville 2004

# M 5b Feed

## M.T. Anderson

In this excerpt, Violet and Titus are chatting about society through their 'feeds'.

1. **Point out** how technological advances affect people's lives.
2. **Characterise** Violet's feelings concerning the 'feed'. Come up with suitable adjectives.
3. Find a partner who has worked on **Text A**. Exchange your results and **discuss** in how far you find the title of the novel appropriate.

And I sat there with my palms pressed into my forehead, thinking about Violet, at home, being smart. I would think about some conversation we were having where I was dumb. Like she was always reading things about how everything was dying and there was less air and everything was getting toxic. She told me about how things were getting really bad with some things in South America, but she couldn't really tell exactly how bad, because the news had been asked to be a little more positive. She said that it made her frightened to read all this kind of things, about how people hated us for what we did. So one time I said to her that she should stop reading it, because it was just depressing, so she was like, *But I want to know what's going on,* so I was like, *Then you should do something about it. It's a free country. You should do something.* She was like, *Nothing's ever going to happen in a two-party system.*

[...]

I thought about that. *We could have everybody vote. From the feeds. Instantaneous*. Then it would be a democracy.*

*Except,* she said, *only about seventy-three percent of Americans have feeds. Oh,* I said. *Yeah.* And so I felt stupid. *There's that many who don't?*

Then she told me, *I didn't use to have a feed.*

I was like, *What do you mean?*

She was quiet like she didn't want to chat. It was that kind of quiet. Then she went, *We didn't have enough money. When I was little. And my dad and mom didn't want me to have one.*

*Holy shit.*

*I got it when I was seven.*

*I'm sorry,* I said.

*For what?*

*For not knowing. You know, that so many people don't have them.*

*No one with feeds thinks about it,* she said. *When you have the feed all you like, you're brought up to not think about things. Like them never telling you that it's a republic and not a democracy. It's something that makes me angry, what people don't know about these days. Because of the feed, we're raising a nation of idiots. Ignorant, self-centered idiots.*

**instantaneous** immediate

M.T. Anderson, *Feed*, Candlewick Press, Somerville 2004

# M6 The Hunger Games

## Suzanne Collins

*The Hunger Games* is a trilogy written by American writer Suzanne Collins. It was published in 2008 and became extremely successful as young adult fiction and received many awards. The story deals with 16-year-old Katniss Everdeen, living in a post-apocalyptic state called *Panem*, which is divided into twelve districts. Once every year, one boy and one girl from each district have to compete against each other in a gladiator-like battle to the death which is televised.
The other two sequels, *Catching Fire* and *Mockingjay*, were published in 2009 and 2010 and have been equally successful.

1. **State** what the excerpt reveals about the antecedents ([ˌæntɪˈsiːd(ə)nt] → sth. that happened or existed before sth. else) leading to the Hunger Games.
2. **Point out** the rules of the Hunger Games.
3. **Explain** how the Hunger Games serve as a means of control over the Districts of Panem.
4. **Examine** which other features of *Panem* are addressed in the excerpt.

At one o'clock, we head for the square. Attendance is mandatory unless you are on death's door. This evening, officials will come around and check to see if this is the case. If not, you'll be imprisoned. [...]
The space gets tighter, more claustrophobic as people arrive. The square's quite large, but not enough to hold District 12's population of about eight thousand. Latecomers are directed to the adjacent streets, where they can watch the event on screens as it's televised live by the state. [...]
Just as the town clock strikes two, the mayor steps up to the podium and begins to read. It's the same story every year. He tells of the story of Panem, the country that rose out of the ashes of a place that was once called North America. He lists the disasters, the droughts, the storms, the fires, the encroaching* seas that swallowed up so much of the land, the brutal war for what little sustenance* remained. The result was Panem, a shining Capitol ringed by thirteen districts, which brought peace and prosperity to its citizens. Then came the Dark Days, the uprising of the districts against the Capitol. Twelve were defeated, the thirteenth obliterated*. The Treaty of Treason gave us the new laws to guarantee peace and, as our yearly reminder that the Dark Days must never be repeated, it gave us the Hunger Games.
The rules of the Hunger Games are simple. In punishment for the uprising, each of the twelve districts must provide one girl and one boy, called tributes, to participate. The twenty-four tributes will be imprisoned in a vast outdoor arena that could hold anything from a burning desert to a frozen wasteland. Over a period of several weeks, the competitors must fight to the death. The last tribute standing wins.
Taking the kids from our district, forcing them to kill each other while we watch – this is the Capitol's way of reminding us how totally we are at their mercy. How little chance we would stand of surviving another rebellion. Whatever words they use, the real message is clear: "Look how we take your children and sacrifice them and there's nothing you can do. If you lift a finger, we will destroy every last one of you. Just as we did in District Thirteen."

**to encroach** to cover more land gradually
**sustenance** food and drink

**to obliterate** to destroy sth. completely

To make it humiliating as well as torturous, the Capitol requires us to treat the Hunger Games as a festivity, a sporting event pitting* every district against the others. The last tribute alive receives a life of ease back home, and their district will be showered with prizes, largely consisting of food. All year, the Capitol will show the winning district gifts of grain and oil and even delicacies like sugar while the rest of us battle starvation. "It is both a time for repentance* and a time for thanks," intones the mayor.

Suzanne Collins, *The Hunger Games*, Klett, Stuttgart 2013, p. 24–26



**to pit against** to make sb. compete or fight against sb. or sth. else

**repentance** the act of showing that you feel ashamed and sorry because you recognize that you have done sth. wrong, especially against the rules of your religion

## M7 The Chrysalids

### John Wyndham

*The Chrysalids*, first published in 1955, is set in a future, post-apocalyptic world in an area roughly equivalent to today's Labrador in Canada. A nuclear war, which people call the "Tribulation" and believe to have been sent by God, has destroyed most of the earth and its inhabitants (the "Old People"), the people of the 20th century. Areas which are still habitable are heavily contaminated with nuclear radiation which is also the reason for a lot of mutations among humans, animals and plants. The people living in this post-nuclear world strongly resemble a rural population living in a village in the 18th century, since no modern technology whatsoever is mentioned. The inhabitants of a village called Waknuk believe that they have to maintain the purity of God's creation (humans, animals, plants) in order to prevent another "Tribulation" and thus their downfall.
The story is told from the perspective of David Strorm, whose father Joseph is the religious patriarch of the village. In this extract, David's Aunt Harriet, who only recently gave birth to a child with a mutation, visits her sister, David's mother, with her child.

1. **Summarise** what the conversation between Aunt Harriet, Emily (David's mother) and Joseph Strorm (David's father) is about.
2. **Point out** why Emily is so aghast about Harriet's proposal to borrow her baby.
3. **Characterise** Aunt Harriet.
4. In the evening, Emily recapitulates the conversation she had with her sister. Put yourself in Emily's shoes and write her diary entry.

@ SNG-40654-001

[...] 'You've got the certificate for her?'
'Of course.' My mother's tone was sharp, ready for offence. I knew the expression which went with the tone. When she spoke again there was a disturbing quality in her voice.
'Harriet!' she demanded sharply. 'Are you going to tell me that you have *not* got a certificate?'
My aunt made no reply, but I thought I caught the sound of a suppressed sob*. My mother said coldly, forcibly*:
'Harriet, let me see that child – properly.'
For some seconds I could hear nothing but another sob or two from my aunt. Then she said, unsteadily:
'It's such a little thing, you see. It's nothing much.'
*'Nothing much!'* snapped my mother. 'You have the effrontery* to bring your monster into my house, and tell me it's nothing much!'

**sob** *Schluchzer*

**forcible** forceful, aggressive

**effrontery** cheekiness, arrogance

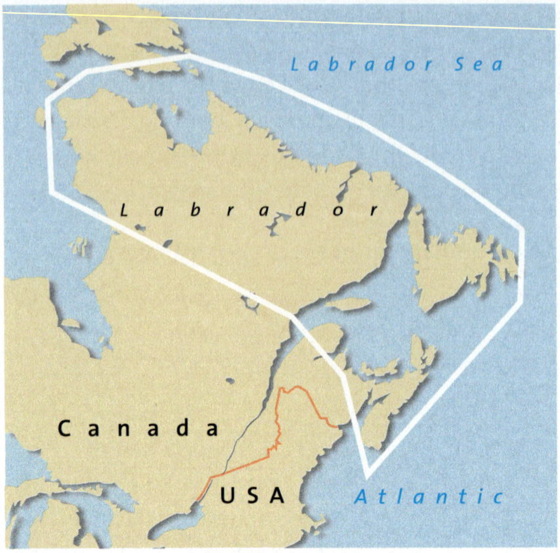


The Waknuk World placed on a present-day map

Book cover from 2008

**moaning** sob

**dull** here: expressionless

**to notify** here: to register, *amtlich mitteilen*

**pointedly** sharply

**incredulous** unbelieving
**words eluded her** *sie konnte nicht die richtigen Worte finden*
**dogged** determined, persistent

**conspiracy** *Verschwörung*

*'Monster!'* Aunt Harriet's voice sounded as though she had been slapped. 'Oh! Oh! Oh! ...' She broke into little moanings*.

After a time my mother said:

'No wonder you didn't dare to call the inspector.'

Aunt Harriet went on crying. My mother let the sobs almost die away before she said:

'I'd like to know why you have come here, Harriet? Why did you bring it here?'

Aunt Harriet blew her nose. When she spoke it was in a dull*, flat voice:

'When she came – when I saw her, I wanted to kill myself. I knew they would never approve her, although it's such a little thing. But I didn't, because I thought perhaps I could save her somehow. I love her. She's a lovely baby – except for that. She is, isn't she?'

My mother said nothing. Aunt Harriet went on:

'I didn't know how, but I hoped. I knew I could keep her for a little while before they'd take her away – just the month they give you before you have to notify*. I decided I must have her for that long at least.'

'And Henry?' What does he say?'

'He – he said we ought to notify at once. But I wouldn't let him – I couldn't, Emily. I *couldn't*. Dear God, not a third time! I kept her, and prayed, and prayed, and hoped. And then when I heard your baby had come early I thought perhaps God had answered my prayers.'

'Indeed, Harriet,' said my mother coldly, 'I doubt whether that had anything to do with it. Nor,' she added pointedly*, 'do I see what you mean.'

'I thought,' Aunt Harriet went on, spiritlessly now, but forcing herself to the words, 'I thought that if I could leave my baby with you, and borrow yours –'

My mother gave an incredulous* gasp. Apparently words eluded* her.

'It would only be for a day or two; just while I could get the certificate,' Aunt Harriet went doggedly* on. 'You are my sister, Emily – my sister, and the only person in the world who can help me to keep my baby.'

She began to cry again. There was another longish pause, then my mother's voice:

'In all my life I have never heard anything so outrageous. To come here suggesting that I should enter into an immoral, a criminal conspiracy* to ... I think you must be mad, Harriet. To think that I should lend –' She broke off at the sound of my father's heavy step in the passage.

'Joseph,' she told him as he entered. 'Send her away. Tell her to leave the house – and take *that* with her.'

'But,' said my father in a bewildered tone, 'but it's Harriet, my dear.'

My mother explained the situation, fully. There wasn't a sound from Aunt Harriet. At the end he demanded incredulously:

'Is this true? Is this why you've come here?'

Slowly, wearily*, Aunt Harriet said:

'This is the third time. They'll take my baby away again like they took the others. I can't stand that – not again. Henry will turn me out, I think. He'll find another wife, who can give him proper children. There'll be nothing – nothing in the world for me – nothing. I came here hoping against hope for sympathy and help. Emily is the only person who can help me. I – I can see now how foolish I was to hope at all ...'

Nobody said anything to that.

'Very well – I understand. I'll go now,' she told them in a dead voice.

My father was not a man to leave his attitude in doubt.

'I do not understand how you dared to come here, to a God-fearing house, with such a suggestion,' he said. 'Worse still, you don't show an atom of shame or remorse.'

Aunt Harriet's voice was steadier as she answered:

'Why should I? I've done nothing to be ashamed of. I am *not* ashamed – I am only beaten.'

'Not ashamed!' repeated my father. 'Not ashamed of producing a mockery* of your Maker – not ashamed of trying to tempt* your own sister into criminal conspiracy!' He drew a breath and launched off in pulpit* style. 'The enemies of God besiege* us. They seek to strike at Him through us. Unendingly they work to distort* the true image; through our weaker vessels* they attempt to defile* the race. You have sinned, woman, search your heart, and you will know that you have sinned. Your sin has weakened our defences, and the enemy has struck through you. You wear the cross on your dress to protect you, but you have not worn it always in your heart. You have not kept constant vigilance* for impurity. So there has been a Deviation*; and deviation, *any* deviation from the true image is blasphemy – no less. You have produced a defilement*.'

'One poor little baby!'

'A baby which, if you were to have your way, would grow up to breed, and, breeding, spread pollution until all around us there would be mutants and abominations*. That is what has happened in places where the will and faith were weak: here it shall *never* happen. Our ancestors were of the true stock: they have handed on a trust. Are you to be permitted to betray us all? To cause our ancestors to have lived in vain? Shame on you, woman! Now go! Go home in humility*, not defiance*. Notify your child, according to law. Then do your penances* that you may be cleansed. And pray. You have much to pray for. Not only have you blasphemed by producing a false image, but in your arrogance you have set yourself against the law, and sinned in intent*. I am a merciful man; I shall make no charge of that. It will be for you to clean it from your conscience; to go down on your knees and pray – pray that your sin of intention, as well as your other sins, may be forgiven you.'

There were two light footsteps. The baby gave a little whimper* as Aunt Harriet picked it up. She came towards the door and lifted the latch*, then she paused.

'I shall pray,' she said. 'Yes, I shall pray.' She paused, then she went on, her voice steady and harder: 'I shall pray God to send charity* into this hideous* world, and sympathy for the weak, and love for the unhappy and unfortunate. I shall ask Him if it is indeed His will that a child should suffer and its soul be damned for a little blemish* of the body ... And I shall pray Him, too, that the hearts of the self-righteous* may by broken ...'

John Wyndham, *The Chrysalids*, Penguin, London 1958, p. 70–73

**weary** tired, exhausted

**mockery** parody, travesty
**to tempt** to persuade, to entice
**pulpit** *Kanzel*
**to besiege** [bɪ'si:dʒ] to encircle, to exert pressure
**to distort** to deform, to falsify
**the weaker vessel** here: *das schwächere Geschlecht*
**to defile** to degrade, to contaminate
**vigilance** guard
**deviation** anomaly
**defilement** degradation, contamination
**abomination** horror

**humility** humbleness, modesty
**defiance** rebellion
**penance** reparation for wrong
**in intent** here: in terms of intention

**whimper** cry
**latch** lock

**charity** kindness
**hideous** dreadful, horrible
**blemish** flaw, imperfection
**self-righteous** *selbstgerecht*

# M 8 "Children of Men": Der Schmerz der ganzen Welt

Andreas Borcholte

The film *Children of Men* from 2006, starring Clive Owen and Julianne Moore and directed by Alfonso Cuarón, is an adaption of P.D. James's novel *Children of Men* and depicts a dystopian society in the year 2027 which has to tackle violence, chaos, ecocide and terrorism. This film review was published on 8 November 2006 in the German online news magazine *SPIEGEL ONLINE Kultur*.

1. Briefly **state** what the film is about, according to the review. Do not take into account the author's opinion here.

2. Imagine visiting a film forum on the Internet. The conversation there is in English and you have only recently read the review about *Children of Men* and it made you curious about it. **Present** the author's overall opinion on the film to the other members of the forum.

3. **Explain** in detail what the author of this review means with "world weariness" and where and how this can be detected in the film.

[...] Den englischen Ausdruck *world weary* würde man wohl am besten mit „lebensmüde“ übersetzen. Weniger Todessehnsucht ist damit gemeint als vielmehr ein generelles Leiden an der Welt, Überdruss* am Alltag, der einen hohläugig* aussehen lässt und tiefe Furchen* durchs Gesicht zieht.

Insofern ist Clive Owen die perfekte Besetzung für Theo, die Hauptfigur in Alfonso Cuaróns Film „Children of Men“. Der britische Schauspieler, unrasiert, verzagt schauend*, in einen abgetragenen* Mantel gekleidet, ist die Personifizierung von *world weary*. Als in der Londoner Fleet Street ein Grill-Imbiss in die Luft fliegt, den Theo gerade eben verlassen hat, verzieht er keine Miene. Terror erzeugt im London des Jahres 2027 keinen Schrecken mehr. Er gehört zum Alltag. [...]

Resignation und Desillusionierung sind nicht nur in Clive Owens Zügen* zu lesen, sie bestimmen den Alltag in der Zukunft: „The World has collapsed; only Britain soldiers on“, propagiert das staatliche Fernsehen in einer Hommage an George Orwell*: Nach dem Kollaps der Welt marschiert nur Großbritannien unverdrossen weiter. Tatsächlich scheint London in der Zukunft von „Children of Men“ die einzige Zuflucht für eine von Krieg und Terror vertriebene Menschheit zu sein. Überschwemmt* von illegalen Immigranten, verlotterten* Gestalten, die an jeder Straßenecke zusammengepfercht* und in militärisch bewachte Hochsicherheits-Auffanglager* abgeschoben* werden, hat sich das Vereinigte Königreich in einen Polizeistaat verwandelt.

Vielleicht soll man es als Strafe Gottes verstehen, vielleicht will aber auch nur die Natur noch größeres Elend verhindern: Die Menschheit in „Children of Men“ ist seit Jahren unfruchtbar*, der jüngste Erdenbürger, ein 18-Jähriger namens Baby Diego, wurde gerade von einem Fanatiker erschossen. Held Theo wollte früher einmal als Polit-Aktivist die Welt verändern. Heute fristet* er als kleiner Beamter einen tristen Büroalltag.

**Überdruss** weariness
**hohläugig** hollow-eyed
**Furche** furrow
**verzagt schauen** to look weak-spirited
**abgetragen** shabby

**Zug** feature

**George Orwell** cf. p. 62

**überschwemmen** to flood
**verlottert** scruffy, gone to rack and ruin
**zusammengepfercht** jammed together
**Hochsicherheits-Auffanglager** maximum-security detention camp
**abschieben** to deport
**unfruchtbar** infertile

**fristen** to lead a miserable existence

Aus seiner Apathie reißt ihn schließlich seine Ex-Frau Julian (Julianne Moore), die sich in der Rebellengruppe „Human Project" engagiert und ihn um Hilfe bittet. Die Beziehung zwischen den beiden erkaltete*, nachdem ihr gemeinsames Kind ums Leben kam. Nun soll Theo ein Mädchen, angeblich eine illegale Immigrantin, an die Küste bringen, wo sie von „Human Project" übernommen werden soll.
Man erfährt nicht, was genau eigentlich die Ziele dieses „Human Project" sind, und die verschlagenen Gestalten in Julians Gefolge erwecken auch nicht gerade viel Vertrauen. Aber sei's drum, es kommt wie es kommen muss: Nach einigen turbulenten, virtuos inszenierten Action- und Verfolgungsszenen [...] sind Theo, das Mädchen Kee und eine Amme* auf sich allein gestellt. Bezeichnenderweise* enthüllt Kee in einem Stall, dass sie – als einzige Frau auf Erden – schwanger ist. Ein Wunder. Und die neue, vielleicht letzte Hoffnung der Menschheit.
Das alles hätte allzu leicht in alt- und neutestamentarisches* Gewaber* abdriften können, wenn nicht Cuarón mit eiserner Hand über den lakonischen*, zuweilen fast dokumentarischen Stil seines Film gewacht hätte: Über weite Strecken wird das Geschehen von einer wackeligen Handkamera gefilmt, als wäre der Kinozuschauer ein Reporter, den es in ein Kriegsgebiet verschlagen hat. Tatsächlich bilden die grünen Landschaften Albions einen krassen Gegensatz zum urbanen Raum, der, so wollte es Cuaròn, an zernarbte* urbane Krisenareale im Kosovo oder Libanon erinnert. In dieser pragmatischen, streng aufs Überleben ausgerichteten Welt, gibt es den Luxus eines Gottes nicht mehr. [...]
Nahezu jeder gesellschaftliche Konflikt unserer Zeit wird in „Children of Men" gestreift*, zum Teil nur en passant*: Da sind die den Folterungen von Abu Ghureib nachgestellten Szenen am Bahnsteig eines Immigrantenlagers, an denen Theo und Kee in einem Zug voller Flüchtlinge vorbeifahren. Da gibt es einen Aufstand bewaffneter muslimischer Terrorgruppen mitsamt „Allah ist mächtig"-Gebrüll, während der Staat der Überalterung* mit der Sterbehilfe*-Pille „Quietus" Einhalt gebieten* will.
Auch die massiven Einschränkungen der Pressefreiheit aus Gründen der „Homeland Security" sind ein Thema: Die unfreiwillig zusammengewürfelten* Flüchtenden, eine schwangere schwarze Einwandererfrau und ein bleicher, resignierter Brite, finden kurzzeitig Unterschlupf bei Theos altem Freund Jasper (Michael Caine), einem Ex-Aktivisten und Alt-Hippie, der heimlich Marihuana raucht und „Ruby Tuesday*" hört. Jaspers Lebensinhalt besteht darin, seine im Rollstuhl sitzende Frau zu pflegen, eine ehemalige Reporterin, die in die Mühlen der Staatsmacht geriet und seitdem im Wachkoma vegetiert.
Es sind die Szenen in Jaspers Landhaus, einer fast weichgezeichneten* Oase der Nostalgie, die „Children of Men" seine Schwere* und Glaubwürdigkeit verleihen. Hier läuft Clive Owen mit Flip-Flops und einem alten verschlissenen* Sweatshirt der Olympischen Spiele von 2012 herum, hier ist ein letzter Rest Humanität und Wärme zu spüren. [...]
Der erste echte Zukunftsthriller des 21. Jahrhunderts verströmt also eine gehörige Portion Retro-Charme. Vielleicht sind es ja wirklich nur noch die Visionen von gestern, die im Morgen Trost spenden. An dieser Aussicht könnte man nun wirklich verzweifeln, wenn „Children of Men" nicht gerade wegen Alfonso Cuaróns Mut zur Anti-Ironie einer der besten und wichtigsten Filme dieses Jahres geworden wäre.

Andreas Borcholte, „Children of Men: Der Schmerz der ganzen Welt", www.spiegel.de, 08.11.2006 [07.02.2014]

**erkalten** to cool down
**Amme** nurse
**bezeichnenderweise** significantly
**alt-/neutestamentarisch** Old and New Testament
**Gewaber** drivel, blather, jabber
**lakonisch** laconical
**zernarbt** scarred
**streifen** to touch on, to deal briefly with
**en passant** incidental
**Überalterung** superannuation of the population
**Sterbehilfe** assisted suicide
**Einhalt gebieten** to curb sth.
**zusammenwürfeln** to throw together
**Ruby Tuesday** song by the Rolling Stones
**weichgezeichnet** blurred
**Schwere** gravity
**verschlissen** worn

**4.** Go to http://en.wikipedia.org/wiki/List_of_dystopian_films for inspiration and choose one dystopian film you would like to write a review about. If you have already watched one, you might write about it as well.

@ SNG-40654-002

**Zoom in: Skills**

## How to write a film review

The purpose of any kind of review is to give the reader a first impression of what the book/film is about and to make a recommendation. It is clearly structured into introduction, main body and conclusion. When writing a review, you should consider the following aspects:

In the introduction you should include

- the film's title;
- the main topic;
- the genre it represents;
- the date and place of release;
- the name of the director.

- *The film is called ...*
- *Its main topic deals with ...*
- *It falls into the category of ...*
- *It was first released in ...*
- *It was directed by ...*

The main body should include

- the setting of the story;
- the main plot of the story;
- the main characters;
- the actors and their performances;
- the cinematic effects, i. e. special effects, music etc.;
- the message of the book/film;
- strengths and weaknesses.

- *The story takes place in .../The plot is laid in .../The scene/action is set in ...*
- *The plot is gripping/thrilling/entertaining/predictable/uninspiring/boring ...*
- *The main characters are well-portrayed/poorly portrayed.*
- *The actors play their roles convincingly/brilliantly/touchingly/weakly/badly/in a mediocre fashion ...*
- *The cinematic devices convincingly reinforce the message of the film.*
- *The book's/film's message directly praises/criticises today's ...*
- *The book's/film's strong aspects/points are ... but it also lacks ...*

In the conclusion you should

- state clearly your own opinion on the book/film;
- say why or why not you would recommend the book/film.

- *In my opinion .../I think that .../As far as I'm concerned ...*
- *I strongly/heartily/enthusiastically recommend reading the book/watching the film because ...*
- *I discourage everyone not interested in ... from reading the book/from watching the film because ...*

adapted from Katharina Einhoff, Powerpack English: *Media literacy*, Schöningh, Paderborn 2011, pp. 100 ff.

# M 9 Fahrenheit 451

## Ray Bradbury

Ray Bradbury's dystopian novel *Fahrenheit 451* can be considered a classic of its genre. First published in 1953, it deals with a totalitarian state in which the burning of books became an instrument of tyranny and censorship. The story is about the fireman Guy Montag, who meets his neighbour Clarisse McClellan. She changes his view and makes him aware of how emotionally reduced his life is due to the lack of books and an oversupply of superficial distraction. Montag starts to question his profession first when an old woman burns herself to death with her books rather than leave her library.
In this extract, Captain Beatty, the captain of the firemen and Montag's boss, gives him an account of the fire brigade's history.

### Zoom in: People

Ray Bradbury

**Ray Bradbury** was born in Illinois on 22 August 1920. In 1934, his family moved to Los Angeles. After having graduated from high school in 1938, Bradbury began writing short stories and by the time he was twenty-three writing was his only profession. He married his wife Marguerite in 1947 and died on 5 June 2012 in Los Angeles.
Bradbury's vision of a totalitarian state, as created in *Fahrenheit 451*, must be seen against the historical background of the Cold War, the ideological antagonism between the western capitalist world and the eastern communist world. Especially during the years 1947 to 1956, communists in the USA had to face political persecution. These years are often referred to as the McCarthy Era, named after Senator Joseph McCarthy who dedicated his life to anti-communist endeavours. The measures employed included for example blacklisting everybody suspected of sympathizing with communism. As a consequence, these people (often artists from the film industry) were prevented from working, which came close to censorship.

1. "There must be something in books, something we can't imagine, to make a woman stay in a burning house; there must be something there. You don't stay for nothing." What makes books special and what makes people die for books in your opinion? Write down your ideas and compare them with your partner.

2. **Outline** the history of the fire brigade as presented by Captain Beatty.

3. **Present** the decline of culture.

4. **Analyse** Captain Beatty's language when explaining the history of the fire brigade to Montag.

5. "Ask yourself, what do we want in this country, above all? People want to be happy, isn't that right? […] Don't we keep them moving, don't we give them fun? That's all we live for, isn't it? For pleasure, for titillation [*Kitzel*]? And you must admit our culture provides plenty of these." (Captain Beatty)
"A room without books is like a body without a soul." (Cicero, Roman author and politician, 106 BC–43 BC) **Contrast** the messages of both quotations.

**to hit sth.** to experience sth.

**to feed it to the rookies** to explain it to beginners
**to let sb. in on sth.** to explain sth. to sb.

**roomy** full of space
**to level down** to make even
**paste pudding norm** *Einheitsbrei*

**cart** vehicle drawn by a horse
**condensation** abridgment, abstract
**digest** summary
**tabloid** *Boulevardzeitung*
**gag** joke
**snap ending** unexpected or sudden ending
**sole** only

**exploiter** *Ausbeuter*
**to fling off** to throw sth. off with force

**to neglect** to disregard, to ignore

**nut** *Schraubenmutter*
**bolt** *Bolzen*
**zipper** *Reißverschluss*

**pratfall** a fall in which one lands on the buttocks

**sauternes** golden-coloured wine from France or California

[...] "When will you be well?"

"Tomorrow. The next day maybe. First of the week."

Beatty puffed his pipe. "Every fireman, sooner or later, hits* this. They only need understanding, to know how the wheels run. Need to know the history of our profession. They don't feed it to rookies* like they used to." Puff. "Only fire chiefs remember it now." Puff. "I'll let you in* on it." [...]

Beatty took a full minute to settle himself in and think back for what he wanted to say. "When did it all start, you ask, this job of ours, how did it come about, where, when? Well, I'd say it really got started around a thing called the Civil War. Even though our rule book claims it was founded earlier. The fact is we didn't get along well until photography came into its own. Then – motion pictures in the early Twentieth Century. Radio. Television. Things began to have *mass*." [...]

"And because they had mass, they became simpler," said Beatty. "Once, books appealed to a few people, here, there, everywhere. They could afford to be different. The world was roomy*. But then the world got full of eyes and elbows and mouths. Double, triple, quadruple population. Films and radios, magazines, books leveled down* to a sort of paste pudding norm*, do you follow me?"

"I think so."

Beatty peered at the smoke pattern he had put out on the air. "Picture it. Nineteenth-century man with his horses, dogs, carts*, slow motion. Then, in the Twentieth Century, speed up your camera. Books cut shorter. Condensations*. Digests*. Tabloids*. Everything boils down to the gag*, the snap ending*." [...]

"Classics cut to fit fifteen-minute radio shows, then cut again to fill a two-minute book column, winding up at last as a ten- or twelve-line dictionary resumé. I exaggerate, of course. The dictionaries were for reference. But many were those whose sole* knowledge of *Hamlet* [...] was a one-page digest in a book that claimed: *now at last you can read all the classics; keep up with your neighbours*. Do you see? Out of the nursery into the college and back to the nursery; there's your intellectual pattern for the past five centuries or more." [...]

"Speed up the film, Montag, quick. *Click, Pic, Look, Eye, Now, Flick, Here, There, Swift, Pace, Up, Down, In, Out, Why, How, Who, What, Where, Eh? Uh! Bang! Smack! Wallop, Bing, Bong, Boom!* Digest-digests, digest-digest-digests. Politics? One column, two sentences, a headline. Then, in mid-air, all vanishes! Whirl man's mind around about so fast under the pumping hands of publishers, exploiters*, broadcasters that the centrifuge flings off* all unnecessary, time-wasting thought!" [...]

"School is shortened, discipline relaxed, philosophies, histories, languages dropped, English and spelling gradually neglected*, finally almost completely ignored. Life is immediate, the job counts, pleasure lies all about after work. Why learn anything save pressing buttons, pulling switches, fitting nuts* and bolts*?" [...]

"The zipper* displaces the button and a man lacks just that much time to think while dressing at dawn, a philosophical hour, and thus a melancholy hour." [...]

"Life becomes one big pratfall*, Montag; everything bang, boff, and wow!" [...]

"Empty the theaters save for clowns and furnish the rooms with glass walls and pretty colors running up and down the walls like confetti or blood or sherry or sauternes*. You like baseball, don't you, Montag?"

"Baseball's a fine game."

Now Beatty was almost invisible, a voice somewhere behind a screen of smoke. [...]

"You like bowling, don't you, Montag?"

"Bowling, yes."

"And golf?"

"Golf is a fine game."

"Basketball?"

"A fine game."

"Billiards, pool? Football?"

"Fine games, all of them."

"More sports for everyone, group spirit, fun, and you don't have to think, eh? Organize and organize and super-organize super-super-sports. More cartoons in books. More pictures. The mind drinks less and less. Impatience. Highways full of crowds going somewhere, somewhere, somewhere, nowhere. The gasoline refugee*. Towns turn into motels, people in nomadic surges* from place to place, following the moon tides*, living tonight in the room where you slept this noon and I the night before." [...]

"Now let's take up the minorities in our civilization, shall we? Bigger the population, the more minorities. Don't step on the toes of the dog-lovers, the cat-lovers, doctors, lawyers, merchants, chiefs, Mormons, Baptists, Unitarians, second-generation Chinese, Swedes, Italians, Germans, Texans, Brooklynites, Irishmen, people from Oregon or Mexico. The people in this book, this play, this TV serial are not meant to represent any actual painters, cartographers, mechanics anywhere. The bigger your market, Montag, the less you handle controversy, remember that! All the minor minor minorities with their ears to be kept clean. Authors, full of evil thoughts, lock up your typewriters*. They *did.* Magazines became a nice blend* of vanilla tapioca*. Books, so the snobbish critics said, were dishwater. No *wonder* books stopped selling, the critics said. But the public, knowing what it wanted, spinning happily, let the comic-books survive. And the three-dimensional sex-magazines, of course. There you have it, Montag. It didn't come from the Government down. There was no dictum*, no declaration, no censorship, to start with, no! Technology, mass exploitation, and minority pressure carried the trick*. Today, thanks to them happy all the time, you are allowed to read comics, the good old confessions*, or trade-journals*."

"Yes, but what about the firemen, then?" asked Montag.

"Ah." Beatty leaned forward in the faint mist of smoke from his pipe. "What more easily explained and natural? With school turning out more runners, jumpers, racers, tinkerers*, grabbers, snatchers, fliers, and swimmers instead of examiners, critics, knowers, and imaginative creators, the word 'intellectual', of course, became the swear word it deserved to be. You always dread* the unfamiliar. Surely you remember the boy in your own school class who was exceptionally 'bright', did most of the reciting and answering while the others sat like so many leaden* idols, hating him. And wasn't it this bright boy you selected for beatings and tortures after hours? Of course it was. We must all be alike. Not everyone born free and equal, as the Constitution says, but everyone *made* equal. Each man the image of every other; then all are happy, for there are no mountains to make them cower*, to judge themselves against. So! A book is a loaded gun in the house next door. Burn it. Take the shot from the weapon. Breach* man's mind. Who knows who might be the target of the well-read man? Me? I won't stomach* them for a minute. And so when houses were finally fire-proofed completely, all over the world [...] there was no longer need of firemen for the old purposes. They were given the new job, as custodians* of our peace of mind, the focus of our understandable and rightful dread of being inferior; official censors, judges, and executors*. That's you, Montag, and that's me."

Ray Bradbury, *Fahrenheit 451*, Cornelsen, Berlin 2005, pp. 51–55



**refugee** person running from sth., often oppression
**surge** wave
**tides** *die Gezeiten*

**typewriter** *Schreibmaschine*
**blend** mixture
**tapioca** food substance prepared from cassava

**dictum** order

**to carry the trick** to achieve sth.
**confession** here: trashy disclosures
**trade-journal** professional journal
**tinkerer** *Bastler/in*

**to dread sth.** to fear sth.

**leaden** ['lɛdn] made of lead

**to cower** to crouch in fear
**to breach** to break, to crack
**to not stomach sb.** to not tolerate sb.
**custodian** caretaker, protector

**executor** *Ausführende/r*

# Genetic Engineering: Horror or Hope?

## M1 Scopes of Genetic Engineering

Science has made great progress in the last fifty years when it comes to exploring the building blocks of life, the genes. Thus, modifying the genes of plants, animals and even humans has developed into a new branch of science, called genetic engineering.

1. Identify the fields represented by the pictures provided. **Explain** which areas of life are affected by genetic engineering.

2. Draw a table with two columns, one for pro arguments and one for counter arguments concerning genetic engineering. Write down at least two arguments in each column. Compare similarities and differences of your results with your partner.

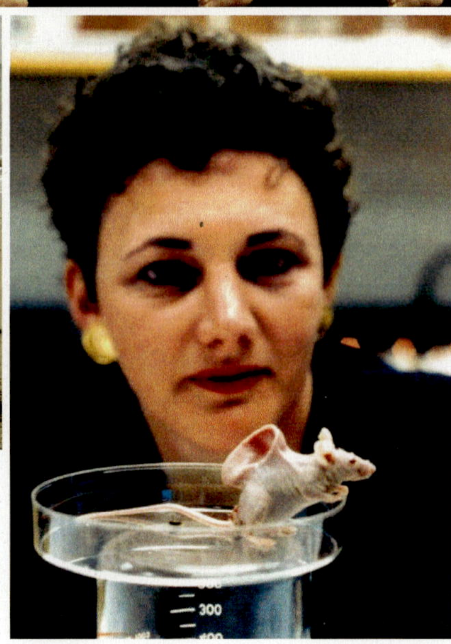

## Zoom in: Terminology

**Genetic engineering** has its origins in genetics, a branch of biology. Biotechnology helps to carry out interventions in the genetic make-up and thus in the biochemical processes affecting all living beings. Genetic engineering refers both to the change/re-combination of DNA sequences in the test tube and in a living organism and the systematic inserting of DNA into living organisms. Genetic engineering is for example applied in agriculture in order to prevent crop failures by making plants resistant to vermin or in pharmaceutics to develop medicines.

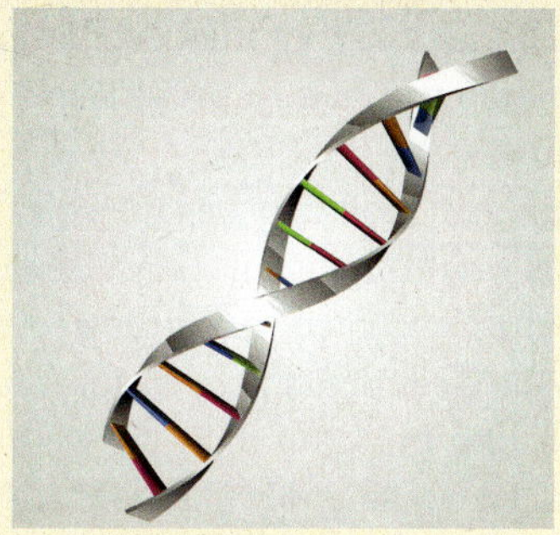

Model of a double helix

In 1980, Paul Berg, Walter Gilbert and Frederick Sanger won the Nobel Prize for Chemistry for having found an efficient method of sequencing DNA. The Human Genome Project, launched in 1990, aimed at completely identifying the human genome. This was finally accomplished in 2003 and the HGP stopped working in 2004. Several other research projects are now concerned with, among other things, finding out about the interaction between different genes when it comes to the outbreak of diseases.

# M 2 Will TPP Open the Door to Frankenstein Food in Japan?

Hugh Ashton

The Internet based news service *Majirox News* covers Japan. This article is about the effects and consequences a Trans-Pacific Partnership (TPP) between Japan and the USA, concerning the import of food, might have.

1. What do you think is meant by "Frankenstein food"?
2. **Describe** what the Trans-Pacific Partnership (TPP) is and what its benefits are.
3. **Analyse** how Ashton gets his message across in respect of his rhetoric.

Genetically modified crops and organisms (GM and GMOs), according to their promoters, offer greater efficiency in production, resistance against disease and pests, and overall greater profitability for all.

On the face of it, this would seem to be ideal for all involved: farmers, food processing companies, and consumers. Inside the United States, according to some sources, GMOs now comprise* two-thirds of the crops grown.

However, there is significant opposition to the introduction of such biotechnology outside the US, especially in Japan, the EU, and Australasia (in 2008, according to the UK's Soil Association, the use of GMOs had cost the US $12 billion in lost exports since 1999). One company, Monsanto, has a large stake* in this aspect of agribusiness*, but suffered a setback in 2003, when the British government released the results of three studies on the effects of GMOs, wherein lasting damage to the environment was predicted if GMOs were introduced.

**to comprise** to make up

**stake** share
**agribusiness** business of agricultural production

In addition, a British poll at that time showed that 93 percent felt that not enough was known about the long-term effects of the so-called GMO Frankenstein food products, and 86 percent saying they would not eat it. This popular reaction and these findings forced an effective halt to Monsanto's research operations in the UK (and in other European centers).

In Japan, food may be labeled as containing GMO ingredients or as being GMO-free, but this would change if a key clause in the Trans-Pacific Partnership (TPP) agreement was to be implemented. According to the Sustainability Council of New Zealand, "the US has made clear that a priority for it in the proposed TPP is the abolition of laws requiring the labeling of GMO food" as well as the acceptance of the import of such products. This clause would apply to the Japanese market and Japanese consumers.

**unwittingly** without fully realizing
**hazard** danger, threat
**ingestion** swallowing
**to sweep under the rug** to conceal sth. in the hopes it will not be discovered by others

If this clause were to be agreed, Japanese consumers would be unwittingly* exposed to any potential health hazards* caused by ingestion* of such food. Critics of the GMO business claim that many such health hazards exist, but that they have been swept under the rug* by the companies involved.

Acceptance of this part of the TPP could also force Japanese farmers to accept the use of GMO crops, which might provide short-term profits. Though even this future profitability is subject to debate (a 2003 study showed that a Monsanto GMO cotton grown in India produced between five and seven times less net income than the indigenous variety according to an official governmental report), introduction of GMOs could bring about dramatic and drastic changes to Japan's ecology – fragile at the best of times.

**imperative** absolutely necessary
**ramification** consequence, implication

It would seem imperative* for the Japanese TPP negotiation team to be well aware of the ramifications* associated with this aspect of the Partnership, and to think carefully before allowing Japanese consumers and the Japanese ecology to be unwittingly exposed to a technology imposed from outside, the effects of which have yet to be objectively and definitively assessed.

Hugh Ashton, "Will TPP open the door to Frankenstein food in Japan?", www.majiroxnews.com, 04.02.2012 [28.10.2013]

## M3 Und dann schuf Gott Monsanto

Jan Grossarth

Monsanto is a US-based company, founded in 1901, which produces seeds and herbicides. Soon after having established a branch for biotechnology in 1981, the company was able to change the genetic code of certain plant parts. Research in this area went on and only two years later Monsanto was the first to have a genetically modified organism patented, in this case a petunia. Today, the company produces transgenic (genetically modified) seeds which are resistant to vermin. However, Monsanto is being criticized for being the only provider for GM seeds, thus having created a monopoly which allows the company to exploit its unique status.

1. What does the headline of this article suggest about the author's attitude towards Monsanto?

2. Briefly **outline** the gist of the article.

3. **Point out** the advantages of GM corn as presented in the article.

**4.** At the end, the article speaks about a farmer who grows strawberries the traditional way without using any kind of GM additive compounds. Put yourself into the shoes of this farmer and together with your partner, write an interview with him in which you reflect about the pros and cons of GM crops.

Monsanto hat schon viele schön-schreckliche Geschichten geliefert. Sie handeln von Korruption und gemeinen Patentklagen*, von gekauften Studien und unheimlichen Vernetzungen des Saatgutkonzerns in die Politik und in die Wissenschaft.
Zusammengenommen kann das ganze kriminalistische Bücher ergeben, die zum Schluss kommen, hier strebe jemand nach Weltmacht und totaler Kontrolle. Ein Monopolist, der sich das Lebensnotwendige patentieren* lässt. Erst am vorletzten Wochenende trieb die Empörung Menschen in vielen hundert Städten auf der Welt auf die Straße. Meist nahmen wenige hundert teil. In Denver zum Beispiel waren es aber mehr als tausend. Sie trommelten in Masken, spielten Gitarre und trugen Schilder, auf denen Totenköpfe und Gasmasken zu sehen waren: „Gentechnik tötet!" Eines illustrierte, wie dem Chef von Monsanto der Kopf abgeschnitten wird.
Der Protest ist nicht neu und kommt nicht zur Ruhe. Aber die Realität hat die Skeptiker und Alarmisten längst eingeholt*. Genmanipulierte Pflanzen, die in Deutschland verboten und politisches Tabuthema sind und nur in Teilen Europas mehr als Zukunftstechnologie denn als Bedrohung wahrgenommen werden – sie dominieren längst hier in Nordamerika. [...]
Bewässerungsgräben* fluten die Felder, Flugzeuge düngen und spritzen. Kalifornien gilt als Gewächshaus* Amerikas – und Amerika ist eines für die halbe Welt. Wie auch deren Experimentierlabor. In Kalifornien, wo die Geschichte der Pflanzengentechnik in den achtziger Jahren im Unternehmen Calgene begann, das später wie viele andere von Monsanto geschluckt wurde, wächst heute kaum noch eine Mais-, Soja- oder Baumwollpflanze, deren Erbgut nicht im Labor verändert wurde. Und für deren Nutzung die Farmer nicht jährlich eine hohe Gebühr* an die Gentech-Konzerne zahlen.

**Der Mais des Grauens**

In den Vereinigten Staaten hat der Anteil genveränderter Organismen (GVO) am Mais, Soja- und Baumwollanbau in diesem Jahr erstmals 90 Prozent erreicht. Die meisten Pflanzen sind gegen Schädlinge* resistent, gegen das Pestizid Glyphosat oder beides. Auch in vielen Entwicklungsländern nehmen die Anbauflächen* stark zu. Die Pflanzen kommen nicht nur von Monsanto – auch aus den Laboren von Pioneer, Syngenta, Bayer, KWS, CAAS aus China oder Nath Seeds aus Indien. Es gibt veränderte Tomaten, Paprika, Papaya. In verarbeiteten Lebensmitteln und als Tierfutter gelangt ein Teil der Ernte ins restriktive Europa, wo nur in wenigen Staaten wenige Sorten angebaut werden.
Der Mais des Grauens, als der er aus deutscher Brille erscheint, spiegelt sich im Wassergraben. Er sieht aus wie gewöhnlicher Mais. Das Feld ist sehr groß. Lastwagen fahren zur Ernte auf und ab. Zwei

**Patentklage** patent lawsuit

**patentieren** to patent

**von der Realität eingeholt werden** to be caught up by reality

**Bewässerungsgraben** irrigation ditch

**Gewächshaus** green house

**Gebühr** fee

**Schädling** pest, vermin

**Anbaufläche** crop area

**Häcksler** shredder
**zerschreddern** to shred
**Halm** stalk, stem, halm
**Maisfetzen** shredded corn
**eingezüchtet** inbred
**Pestizid** pesticide
**im Angebot** on offer
**Reagenzglas** test tube
**Trockenheit** drought [draut]
**durchschnittlich** average
**Ernte** harvest
**stiften** to donate
**Stipendium** scholarship
**jdn. belehren** to instruct
**Ertrag** here: crop yield
**trockenresistent** drought-resistant
**Züchtung** breeding

Häcksler* rattern durch die Felder. Vom Fahrersitz sieht es so aus, als steure die Maschine auf eine grüne Wand zu, so hoch sind die Pflanzen. Der Häcksler zerschreddert* die Halme* der Sorte MON88913 und spuckt die Maisfetzen* auf die Ladefläche der nebenherfahrenden Lastwagen. Maisstaub liegt wie Nebel in der Luft. Ein Mexikaner, Saisonarbeiter, sitzt am Steuer. Er sagt, er mache sich keinen Kopf. Sei alles normal: „Ich liebe Gentechnik", lacht er, „no problem."

Man kann lange suchen, bis man in Amerika einen Bauern oder Landarbeiter findet, der ein schlechtes Wort über die GVO sagt. [...] „Unser Mais? Na klar, er ist genverändert. Das ist hier längst kein Thema mehr." Die Ernten seien besser, die Kosten geringer, weil er für die Genpflanzen, die eingezüchtete* Resistenzen enthalten, ein Drittel weniger Pestizide* kaufen müsse.

Die Farmer kaufen ihr Saatgut von Monsanto, weil ihnen dann am Ende des Jahres deutlich mehr Geld auf dem Konto bleibt. [...]

**Es gibt kein Monopol und keinen Zwang**

Das wird im Supermarkt deutlich – hier, irgendwo am Stadtrand vom Omaha, der Hauptstadt Nebraskas. Popcorn ist im Angebot*. Auf der Verpackung steht kein Hinweis auf genveränderte Zutaten. Nicht mal „Mais" steht auf der Zutatenliste: „Enthält Popcorn, Rapsöl, Honig, Salz." Die Verpackungen von Tortilla-Chips, aus Mais und frittiert im Sojaöl, sind mit „all natural" bedruckt.

Es gibt kein Monopol und keinen Zwang, außer der Lust auf Gewinne. Das sagt auch Tom Petersen, ein Maisbauer der vierten Generation unweit von Omaha. Er findet nur Gutes an den immer neuen Pflanzensorten aus dem Reagenzglas*. Es geht nicht nur um Einsparungen. „Im Vergleich mit 1980 ernten wir hier doppelt so viel Mais pro Acre Land. Die Verkaufspreise haben sich in zehn Jahren verdoppelt. Wir verdienen hier richtig gutes Geld."

Tom und sein greiser Vater Don, der nach dem Weltkrieg eine Weile als Soldat in Frankfurt lebte, bauen in diesem Jahr auch erstmals Mais an, der im Labor so verändert wurde, dass er nicht nur Schädlingen und Spritzmitteln, sondern auch Trockenheit* widerstehen soll. Wenn das funktioniert, sollte das die durchschnittlichen* Ernten* erhöhen. [...]

Nahe San Francisco steht das Zentrum für Pflanzenforschung der Universität Davis. Wie üblich, wird diese teils von der Industrie finanziert. Monsanto stiftet* Stipendien*. Am Konferenztisch sitzt die wissenschaftliche Mannschaft, führende Forscher. Auch sie werden schnell emotional, wenn es um Gentechnik geht. Ein Protokoll:

Eduardo Blumwald, Professor für Zellbiologie: „Es wurde jetzt eine Generation mit GVO ernährt. Wie viele wurden davon krank? Nicht einer. Ihr Europäer glaubt, ihr seid schlauer. Ja, ja: die dummen Amerikaner! Ach was: Eure Chemieindustrie ist mächtig. Die will keine GVO, denn die schadet dem Geschäft."

Alan Bennett, Professor für Pflanzenforschung: „Ihr Europäer belehrt* uns immer bezüglich des Klimawandels: Amerikaner, hört endlich auf die Wissenschaft! Und wenn es um GVO geht, hört Ihr selbst nicht auf die Wissenschaft. Ich kenne keinen Wissenschaftler, der nicht für die Gentechnik wäre. Außer einem in Berkeley. Aber der ist kein Wissenschaftler."

**Warum geben sie es bitte für Kampagnen aus?**

Kent Bradford, Direktor für Saatgut-Biotechnologie: „Greenpeace hat ein höheres Budget, als der amerikanische Staat für Forschung in der Pflanzengenetik ausgibt. Warum geben sie es bitte für Kampagnen aus? Warum nicht dafür, die Pflanzen zu verbessern? Die Erträge* müssen steigen, sonst gibt es bald wieder mehr Hunger auf der Welt. Stattdessen zerstören die Aktivisten Felder."

In einem Aufsatz schreibt Alan Bennett, was bald kommen werde: Pflanzen mit neuen Vitaminen, viele trockenresistente* Züchtungen*, genveränderte Fische.

Etwas weiter im Landesinneren von Kalifornien, nahe der Kleinstadt Yuba City mit ihren

Walnuss- und Tomatenplantagen, bewirtschaftet ein Einwanderer aus den Philippinen mit einem uralten Traktor zwei Hektar. Er baut gewöhnliche Erdbeeren an und verkauft sie an der Straße. Davon ernährt er seine Frau und vier Kinder. Sie leben in einer Holzhütte. Er sagt, die steigenden Pachtpreise* machten ihm zu schaffen*. Er sieht glücklich aus. Sein Nachbar, ein Farmer, muss über ihn den Kopf schütteln: „So wie der wird man die Welt nicht ernähren können."

Jan Grossarth, „Und dann schuf Gott Monsanto", www.faz.net, 17.10.2013 [28.10.2013]

**Pachtpreis** price for the rent
**zu schaffen machen** to cause sb. difficulties

## M4 Genetic Modification: Glow-In-The-Dark Lifesavers or Mutant Freaks?

Robin McKie

This article, published in the British daily newspaper *The Guardian* on 8 August 2010, deals with the benefits and dangers of transgenic animals.

1. Try to anticipate arguments for viewing transgenic animals as "glow-in-the-dark lifesavers" or "mutant freaks". Compare your arguments with those of a partner.
2. **Present** the author's arguments in favour of and against GM animals and compare them with your ideas from task 1.
3. How does McKie try to convince the reader of his opinion? **Analyse** the article and concentrate on the author's strategy when it comes to appearing credible to his readers.

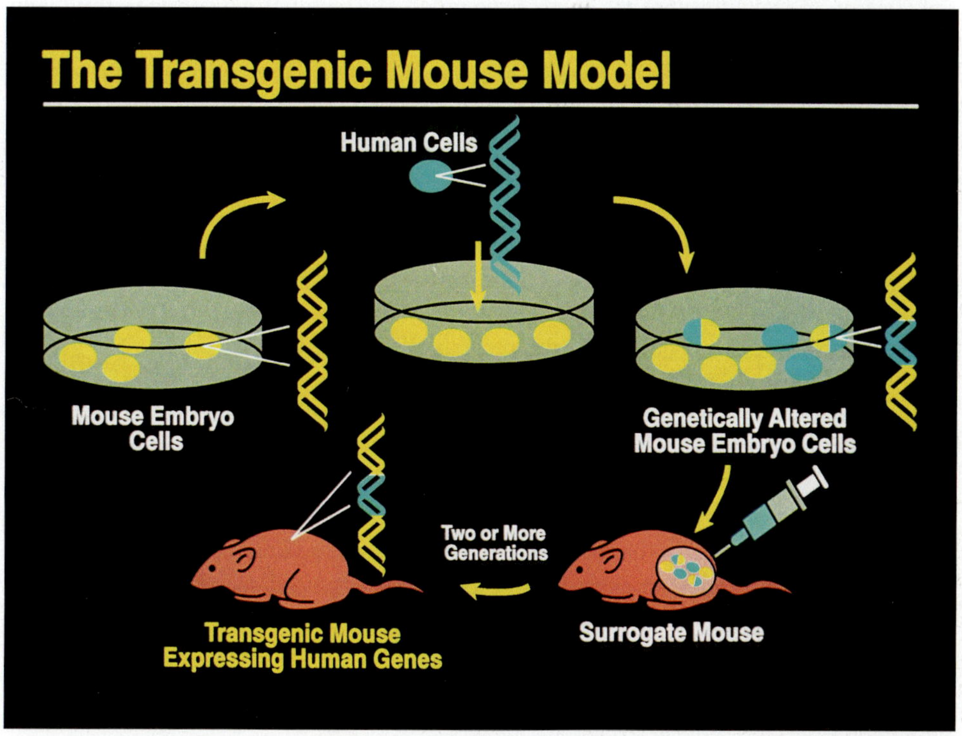

**to fluoresce** [flʊ'rɛs] to glow in the dark
**hue** colour tone
**poultry** *Geflügel*

At first glance, the creation of a chicken that glows in the dark seems a disturbing and unnecessary one. With a jellyfish gene inserted into its DNA, a hen modified this way acquires the power to fluoresce* in a bright green hue* when illuminated with blue light – an unsettling ability, to say the least. After all, who needs poultry* that can shine a light on itself? More important, why go to the trouble of mixing the DNA of two such dissimilar creatures in the first place?

It is an important question that has recently been reflected in headlines that followed the release of Home Office figures which show there was a dramatic rise in the creation of genetically modified animals in laboratories in 2009. In total, 1.5m experiments on GM animals were carried out, a rise of 143,000 from the previous year. At the same time, there was a corresponding decrease in experiments on "natural" animals.

In other words, more and more scientists are now relying on the use of GM animals, as opposed to unmodified ones, for their research. But what gives the insertion of a piece of DNA from one living being into another such an advantage for scientists? After all, inserting invertebrate* genes into mammals*, and vice versa, is not easy. It also makes the public uncomfortable and raises the hackles* of animal rights organisations. Yet it has become the standard route for researchers. Why?

**invertebrate** *wirbelloses Tier*
**mammal** animal that feeds milk to its young and that usually has hair or fur covering most of its skin
**to raise hackles** to enrage sb.
**Dolly the sheep** the first cloned mammal

Consider that glowing poultry. Fluorescent chickens were developed by scientists at Edinburgh University's Roslin Institute, the zoological research organisation responsible for the creation of Dolly the sheep*. As we have noted, the technique involves putting jellyfish genes into the DNA of a chick so that it makes a green, fluorescent protein. "The protein itself does not affect the chicken in any way but it is a very useful tool for looking at the very early embryos," says Roslin researcher Professor Helen Sang.

The crucial point is that chicks are extremely useful for studying embryo development because their growth takes place inside an egg which can be kept in an incubator and studied fairly easily. By contrast, a mammal foetus gestates* inside the uterus of its mother, making it far harder for researchers to monitor* physiological changes. Thus the chick provides us with a key model for understanding the development of early embryos for all vertebrates*, including humans. But the technique had been pushed to its limits by scientists – until the arrival of the GM mutant. This allows scientists to tinker with* the way in which an embryo develops and so reveal processes that were previously obscured*.

**to gestate** to develop in the womb
**to monitor** to watch carefully
**vertebrate** *Wirbeltier*
**to tinker with** to fiddle with, to play with
**to obscure** to conceal, to hide

"You can take a sample of cells from a green embryo and then put them into a normal embryo," says Sang. "You can then watch and see what organ that group of cells develops into because that tissue will have a green fluorescence. For example, if this part of the chick embryo develops into stem cells, that tells us whether other animals, including humans, have stem cells in that part of their embryos and will therefore provide us with important basic biological insights." In other words, stem-cell science can get a boost from the glowing green chicken.

In fact, the chicken turns out to be a popular target for modification. Roslin scientists are also working on a strain that can express therapeutic proteins in the whites of eggs. In particular, they are working on whites in which the hen expresses antibodies that can block viruses which cause enteric* – i. e. gut* – diseases. Thus it may be possible one day to cook omelettes that could prevent us succumbing to disease*, though most scientists envisage a slightly different route in which GM egg whites are dried out before their antibodies are removed and administered* separately.

But what geneticists have not developed, insists Sang, is the featherless chicken, [...]. This animal is often held up as the ultimate GM horror, created so that farmers will be saved the effort of having to pluck feathers before poultry are sold to supermarkets. In fact, the partly featherless chicken is a species containing a natural mutation called naked neck which is becoming popular in hot countries, such as Israel, where the animals can be kept cool without a full feather covering.

Nevertheless, there are other criticisms of the use of GM animals, as the watchdog group GeneWatch has pointed out. Its director Helen Wallace says the rise in the use of GM animals reveals a disturbing trend: the "genetification" of biology. "There are undoubtedly some legitimate uses of GM animals but this blanket* rise is worrying and bears little relation to reality," she says. Wallace points to the widespread creation of animals – mice in particular – that have been genetically altered so they succumb to human conditions such as obesity and cancer. These mutants are then used to test drugs that could counter these ailments* in humans.

"The trouble with this approach is that it stresses the use of medical intervention for ailments that also have clear environmental causes," says Wallace. "Too much food and exposure* to pollutants are also clear causes of cancer and obesity, but these are being ignored because of our obsession with genetics. In fact, in many conditions, genes have only a small role to play in the causation of the disease, yet we have become fixated on trying to tackle them, to the detriment* of other, more fruitful approaches."

This point is acknowledged – partially – by genetic engineers. "We do concentrate a lot on genetic approaches to disease, but that is because we geneticists are only now catching up with other sciences," says Luke Alphey, head of Oxitec, an Oxford University spin-off genetics company. "For the first time, we have got the tools to do this sort of thing. And in any case, a disease is generally a combination of genetic and environmental causes. So the more we learn about genetic influences the more we will know about their environmental influences as well."

Alphey and his colleagues are working on techniques to prevent mosquitoes from spreading dengue fever, a severe, sometimes fatal viral illness that affects between 50 to 100 million people a year. "We have created a strain of genetically modified male mosquitoes of the *Aedes aegypti* species, the one responsible for spreading dengue fever," he says. "These males produce offspring that do not develop fully. So they block the appearance of new *A. aegypti* mosquitoes. Released into the wild, which we hope to do in a few years, these GM mosquitoes should eradicate *A. aegypti* populations and halt* new dengue fever cases. If the technique works, we will have demonstrated just how powerful and useful this technology can be."

Robin McKie, "Genetic modification: glow-in-the-dark lifesavers or mutant freaks?", www.theguardian.com, 08.08.2010 [05.11.2013]

**enteric** pertaining to the stomach
**gut** stomach
**to succumb to disease** to die from a disease
**to administer** here: to give or apply
**blanket** widespread
**ailment** disorder, illness
**exposure** the condition of being exposed to something
**detriment** disadvantage
**to halt** to stop

**4.** Stage a formal debate with the motion "GM animals – a benefit to the human race or man-made monsters?" The debate should comprise of at least three speakers in favour of GM animals and three speakers against GM animals.

# M5 Is Ethical Human Genetic Enhancement Possible?

Alex Knapp

The American *Forbes Magazine* is one of the most famous magazines dealing with the economy and economic issues in general. In his article, journalist Alex Knapp raises the question whether ethical human genetic enhancement is possible.

1. "Ethical human genetic enhancement is possible if ..." Complete the sentence with at least three arguments.
2. **Outline** the author's argumentation and compare it with your initial idea.
3. **Illustrate** how Knapp tries to convince his readers of his opinion. Focus on his line of argument in particular.
4. **Comment** on the author's conclusion that he does not "think it's possible to get there without committing horrific moral atrocities" (l. 75 f.).

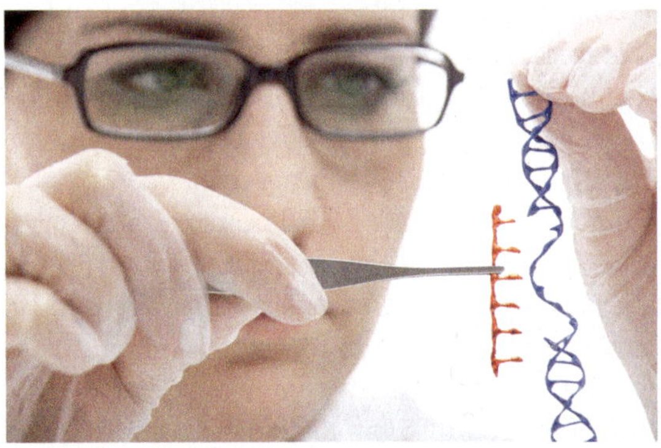

[...] But one thing that I find interesting about the discussion is this kind of baseline assumption that humans will be capable of genetic engineering that makes people smarter, stronger, faster, healthier, longer-lived, etc.

From my perspective though, there's a lot of logistics being hand-waved away in this discussion. *How*, exactly, do we expect human genetic enhancement to *happen*?

Obviously, some types of human genetic engineering are possible. Gene therapy, for example, is promising for some genetic conditions, but it typically involves adding new cells to the body (in particular, the bone marrow*). It doesn't require rewriting someone's DNA wholesale*. And frankly, rewriting an adult's DNA from the ground up presents so many technical difficulties that I think it's safe to say that it's probably impossible.

It's precisely because that technical issue exists that most discussions of human genetic engineering tend to revolve around* human embryos. And here's where the ethical issues arise. Simple genetic engineering – changing one gene – is probably pretty technically straightforward and doesn't pose too many thorny issues. For example, an embryo with phenyketonuria (a rare genetic disorder) only needs one gene corrected to develop into a healthy baby. (Though this is still *way* easier said than done.)

But when we move beyond dealing with just one gene, and into enhancing more complex systems, we enter a different world of ethical and technical issues.

**bone marrow** a soft substance that fills the bones of people and animals
**wholesale (adv.)** on a large scale
**to revolve around sth.** to centre around, to focus on

### The Complexity of Biological Systems

Let me steal a few points from my earlier essay about the ethics of animal enhancement, because those issues are even more prevalent* here. Let's start with the most common dream of transhumanism – making people significantly more intelligent. Here's the thing about human intelligence – it's incredibly complex. The brain is an amazingly com-

**prevalent** widespread

plicated organ that we're only just now starting to understand. But there are a few things that we do know, and one of those things is that intelligence is almost certainly polygenic – meaning that there are many, many genes that underlie human intelligence. So making babies smarter isn't as simple as just expressing one or two genes. It means changing an entire system. So it's a daunting* task to achieve Kyle Munkittrick's stated assumption of transhumans with "genetic profiles allowing IQs above 200."

**daunting** frightening, intimidating

Now, exactly what we'd need to do to increase intelligence to that level is fairly speculative, but we can make a few educated guesses. For this type of superintelligence, where the average transhuman isn't just on the right side of the intelligence bell curve*, but actually OFF of it, we're going beyond just copying and pasting Einstein's brain and calling it a day*. We would probably have to increase the size of the brain to increase the brain/body ratio* and pack in more neurons. We would probably alter the structures of portions of the brain to achieve desired traits. That's hard enough – but now think of what we need to support that. More neurons mean higher energy and oxygen requirements – meaning that increasing intelligence likely *also* means altering the metabolic and respiratory systems*. We would also probably have to alter hormonal regulation, since a larger, differently structured brain will probably also need different levels of various hormones. Also, if we're making the brain bigger, we have to make the head bigger. Which means we have to make the spine stronger. And so on.

**bell curve** here: normal distribution

**to call it a day** to stop

**ratio** proportion

**metabolic system** *Stoffwechsel*
**respiratory system** *Atemwege*

Of course, my educated guess about how intelligence enhancement might come about could be wrong. But what I doubt I'm wrong about is the need to change an extraordinary number of genes and biological systems in order to provide the changes needed to support genetic "superintelligence." Assuming, of course, that such intelligence is even physically possible. (And that's just talking about the genetic component, which isn't all there is to intelligence by a long shot*.)

**not by a long shot** *bei Weitem nicht*

**The Inevitable Consequences**

The bottom line being, if we're talking about significant genetic changes to human beings, whether it's making people smarter or stronger or able to fly or whatever, we're talking about making changes to extraordinarily complex systems – all at once. Those changes will almost certainly have to be made on the embryonic level, and those embryos will grow into babies. And only once they're born will we even know if the "enhancement" actually worked as planned. Of course, as any engineer will tell you, the more complex the system, the more testing is required. The more testing required, the more prototypes are made. Most of them failures. Only in the case of human genetic enhancement, the tests are performed on people. The "failed prototypes" are people. People who have to grow up and live with the consequences of the *inevitable* mistakes that will be made in the process of experimenting. Assuming, of course, they can physically live with those consequences at all. And there's the problem. When you get right down to it, I do not see any way to perform experiments involving significant genetic enhancements that don't end in the suffering of a human being. A human being whose DNA was altered without consent, who is participating in a scientific experiment without consent, and is, basically, being born into slavery, with their sole purpose in life being a stepping stone to making *other* people "better."

He also compared it to slavery whe he said they were

Human genetic enhancement may be technically possible, but given what we know about biology, I don't think it's possible to get there without committing horrific moral atrocities*.

**atrocity** a very cruel or terrible act or action

Alex Knapp, "Is Ethical Human Genetic Enhancement Possible?", www.forbes.com, 15.09.2011 [28.10.2013]

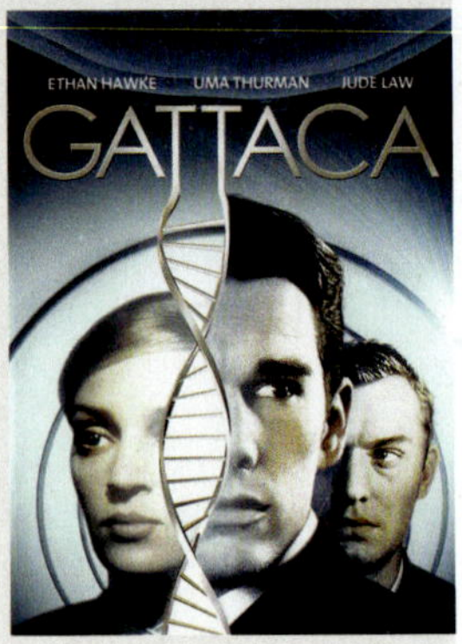


# M6 Gattaca

## Andrew M. Niccol

The film *Gattaca* depicts a future society in which genes predetermine the social status and the individual's path of life. Vincent Freeman (the protagonist) is genetically "invalid" (cf. screenplay) and takes on the identity of Jerome Morrow, a "valid" person, in order to fulfil his dream of travelling to Titan, a distant planet. Vincent/Jerome works at *Gattaca*, an aeronautics and space organization.
The beginning of the film introduces the audience to the world and society of *Gattaca* and provides insights into Vincent's childhood.

1. **Point out** how the importance of one's genes is reflected.

2. **Analyse** how Vincent's parents react to the diagnosis of the geneticist after his birth.

**Ext.** exterior, outside

**VO** voice-over

**Int.** interior, inside

**stirrup** Steigbügel

**adamant** determined not to change your belief or decision about something

**Part II**

EXT.* BEACH. DUSK – THIRTY-ODD YEARS EARLIER

A starry sky. The camera tilts down to find palm trees swaying against a setting sun.

JEROME (VO*) *I was conceived in the Riviera. Not the French Riviera.*

The camera tilts down further to find a Buick Riviera parked in a deserted beachfront parking lot on a polluted stretch of beach.

JEROME (VO) *The Detroit variety.*

Through the car's steamed windows we see Jerome's mother and father, MARIA and ANTONIO, early twenties, making love.

JEROME (VO) *They used to say that a child conceived in love, has a greater chance of happiness. They don't say that any more.*

INT.* FAMILY PLANNING CLINIC. DAY.

MARIA, wearing a medical gown, lies on an examining table, feet in stirrups*. A NURSE, forties, wheels an instrument tray towards her. Maria suddenly disengages her feet from the stirrups and swings her legs off the table.

NURSE *What are you doing?*

MARIA (shaking her head) *I can't do this.*

NURSE (misinterpreting the problem) *I told you, the government pays. It's all taken care of.*

MARIA *No, you don't understand. I can't.*

The nurse places a comforting hand on Maria's shoulder.

NURSE (reassuring) *The doctor will give you something.*

MARIA (removing the hand, adamant*) *I'm not doing it.*

NURSE (trying to make her see reason) *Honey, you've made one mistake –*

The remark stings Maria.

NURSE (softening her tone) – *I've read your profile. I don't know about the father but you carry enough hereditary factors on your own.*

(pause)

*You can have other children.*

MARIA (holding her swollen stomach protectively) *Not like this one.*

NURSE (trying to be diplomatic) *Honey, look around you. The world doesn't want one like that one.*

Maria gets off the table and reaches for her clothes laying across a chair.

MARIA (irate*) *You don't know what it will be!*

The nurse watches Maria as she dresses, genuinely bewildered*.

NURSE (calling out to Maria as she disappears out of the door) *The child won't thank you!*

INT. DELIVERY ROOM. DAY.

We focus on a crucifix dangling on a rosary*. Tilting up we find the rosary clasped between MARIA and ANTONIO's intertwined hands.

JEROME (VO) *Those were early days – days when a priest could still persuade someone to put their faith in God's hands rather than those of the local geneticist.*

Bathed in sweat, Maria gives a final push on the delivery table.

While still attached to his umbilical cord*, the heel of the NEWBORN BABY BOY is immediately pricked by a masked NURSE. A minute drop of blood is inserted into an analyzing machine.

Even as the baby is put into Maria's arms, page after page of data begins to appear on a monitor, pulsing warning signals throughout the spreadsheets.

Two assisting NURSES exchange a look. Antonio senses something amiss.

ANTONIO *What's wrong?*

JEROME (VO) *Of course, there was nothing wrong with me. Not so long ago I would have been considered a perfectly healthy, normal baby. Ten fingers, ten toes. That was all that used to matter. But now my immediate well-being was not the sole concern.*

Antonio turns his attention from his baby to the data appearing on the monitor. We see individual items highlighted amongst the data – "NERVE CONDITION – PROBABILITY 60%", "MANIC DEPRESSION – 42%", "OBESITY – 66%", "ATTENTION DEFICIT DISORDER – 89%" –

JEROME (VO) *My destiny was mapped out before me – all my flaws, predispositions* and susceptibilities* – most untreatable to this day. Only minutes old, the date and cause of my death was already known.*

Antonio focuses on a final highlighted item on the monitor's screen, "HEART DISORDER – 99% – EARLY FATAL POTENTIAL".
"LIFE EXPECTANCY – 33 YEARS".

Andrew M. Niccol, Gattaca. A Screen Play, www.imsdb.com [16.12.2012]

**irate** very angry

**bewildered** [bɪ'wɪldə(r)d] confused and not certain what to do

**rosary** *Rosenkranz*

**umbilical cord** *Nabelschnur*

**predisposition** *Veranlagung*
**susceptibility** (to) *Anfälligkeit (für)*

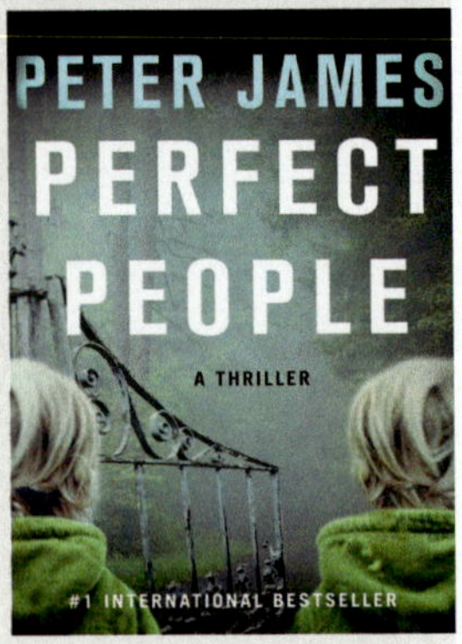


# M7 Perfect People

Peter James

John Klaesson and his wife Naomi are grieving the death of their four-year-old son from a rare genetic disorder. In this excerpt from the novel, they are consulting geneticist Dr Leo Dettore who has methods that can spare the heartache of ever losing a child to any disease.

1. Have a look at the book cover provided. How does it make you feel? **Describe** its atmosphere.
2. **Outline** Dr Dettore's argumentation in favour of genetically enhancing human offspring as well as Klaesson's reservations about the whole idea.
3. **Analyse** the means the geneticist uses to convince the couple of having the genes of their future child enhanced. Pay specific attention to his line of argument, the use of rhetorical devices, and his body language, as described in the extract.
4. Naomi Klaesson is deeply worried about "this whole eugenics thing" (l. 44). **Discuss** the implications of genetic enhancement as presented in this excerpt.
5. From Naomi Klaesson's point of view, write a letter to Dr Dettore, either accepting or rejecting his offer to enhance your child's genes.

**Zoom in: Vocabulary**

**düster** gloomy, dismal • **neblig** foggy, misty • **beklemmend** nightmarish, oppressive • **bedrohlich** threatening, menacing

Dettore sat upright, folded his arms and rocked back and forward a few times, like a big child himself. 'Naomi, I hear what you're saying. You want your kid to be just a regular guy with corners of talent and occasional brilliance, right?'

'I – I suppose, yes. Exactly.'

'I'd go along with that, except there is one thing you have to take into account. You have to compare a model of the world today, with a model of what the world will be like when your son becomes an adult. You're twenty-eight years old, and the world is not substantially different to when you were a little girl. But, in twenty-eight years' time?' He opened his arms expansively. 'I'm telling you that in twenty-eight years' time the world *will* be different. There will be a genetic underclass that will create a divide bigger than you can imagine. You compare the knowledge, skills, advantages you have right now over some poor young woman your age brought up in the Third World, working on a paddy field* in China, or maybe in the bush in Angola.'

Dettore stood up, went over to his desk and tapped his computer keyboard for some moments. A map of the world appeared on the large wall screen opposite them. There were some pink blotches, but mostly the countries were in white.

'There are seven billion people in the world. Do you know how many of them can read or write?' He looked at John, then Naomi.

'No,' she said. 'I don't.'

'If I tell you that twenty-three per cent of adults in the United States, the most technologically advanced nation in the world, are illiterate, does that give you any clues? Forty-four million who cannot read in the *United States*, for heaven's sakes! It's less than a bil-

**paddy field** a field in which rice is grown in water

lion in the whole world who can. Less than twenty per cent. Just those pink areas on the map. The average rural dweller* in the Third World receives less information in his or her entire lifetime than is contained in one issue of the *LA Times*.'

A phone rang; he glanced down at it, then ignored it and after a few moments it stopped. 'Naomi,' he said gently, 'you may not be comfortable with this fact, but you are already a member of a master-race. I don't think you'd want to go trade places with too many other people on this planet. I don't think you'd want your child to be brought up on the Russian steppes, or in a Himalayan tea plantation, or some settlement out in the Gobi Desert. Am I right?'

'Of course.'

'But you'd be prepared to take the risk that your son ends up in a kind of intellectual Third World?'

She looked at him and said nothing.

'These are early days,' Dettore said. 'In thirty years' time, all children from families or nations that can afford it are going to be genetically enhanced*. You see the options you have on that list we're working through? At the moment they are just options, but when you start living in a world where every expectant mother is ticking her way through that same list, are you going to leave all the boxes blank? No way! Not unless you want to have a totally disadvantaged kid – one who won't be able to keep up or compete in the world.'

'I'll tell you what really worries me about this whole thing – and I know it worries John, too, because we've discussed this endlessly over the past months, since you accepted us, and it's this' – she shrugged – 'this whole *eugenics** thing. It has a bad history, bad associations.'

Dettore perched on the edge of his desk and leaned towards Naomi. 'If we human beings never try to improve the genes of our offspring because eighty years ago a madman called Mr Hitler tried to do it, then in my opinion we may have won the Second World War, but Mr Hitler will have won the peace that followed.' He looked very solemn. 'Edward Gibbon wrote, *All that is human must retrograde* if it does not advance*. He was right. Any civilization, any generation that does not advance will eventually decline*.'

'And didn't Einstein say that if he had known that the consequences of his work would have led to the atom bomb, he would have become a watchmaker instead?' Naomi said.

'Sure,' Dettore said. 'And if Einstein had become a watchmaker, we might today be living in a world where Hitler's eugenics was our future.'

'Instead of yours?' Naomi said. Instantly she regretted the remark. I'm sorry,' she said. 'I didn't mean –'

'I think what she's saying is that it's one perspective against another,' John butted in quickly.

'It's OK, it's a valid point,' Dettore said. 'Plenty of people have made the comparison. I've been called the Antichrist, a Neo-Nazi, Dr Frankenstein, you name it. I just hope I have more humanity than Mr Hitler did. And maybe a little more humility, too.'

Peter James, *Perfect People*, Pan Macmillan, London 2012, pp. 34–36

**rural dweller** a person that lives in the countryside

**to enhance** to improve

**eugenics** [juːˈdʒenɪks] the study of methods to improve the mental and physical abilities of the human race by choosing who should become parents

**to retrograde** return to an earlier and worse situation

**to decline** decrease in quantity or importance

# M 8 Brave New World: Kazuo Ishiguro's Novel Really Is Chilling

Margaret Atwood

The title of this book review refers to Aldous Huxley's most famous dystopian novel *Brave New World*, published in 1932. Margaret Atwood herself is a famous Canadian author and poet. She received numerous awards and prizes for her work (cf. p. 13).
This review was published on 1 April 2005.

1. **Point out** how, according to Atwood, Ishiguro made use of extrapolation in his novel (to extrapolate = to predict by projecting past experience or known data).
2. **Examine** Atwood's attitude towards *Never Let Me Go*. Focus on tone and language, also taking the headline into account.

Film poster

*Never Let Me Go* is the sixth novel by Kazuo Ishiguro [...]. It's a thoughtful, crafty, and finally very disquieting look at the effects of dehumanization on any group that's subject to it. In Ishiguro's subtle hands, these effects are far from obvious. There's no Them-Bad, Us-Good preaching; rather there's the feeling that as the expectations of such a group are diminished, so is its ability to think outside the box it has been shut up in. The reader reaches the end of the book wondering exactly where the walls of his or her own invisible box begin and end. [...]

The narrator, Kathy H., is looking back on her school days at a superficially idyllic establishment called Hailsham. [...] At first you think the "H" in "Kathy H." is the initial of a surname, but none of the students at Hailsham has a real surname. Soon you understand that there's something very peculiar about this school. [...]

In fact, Hailsham exists to raise cloned children who have been brought into the world for the sole purpose of providing organs to other, "normal" people. They don't have parents. They can't have children. Once they graduate, they will go through a period of being "carers" to others of their kind who are already being deprived of their organs; then they will undergo up to four "donations" themselves, until they "complete." [...] The whole enterprise, like most human enterprises of dubious morality, is wrapped in euphemism and shadow. The outer world wants these children to exist because it's greedy for the benefits they can confer*, but it doesn't wish to look head-on at what is happening. We assume – though it's never stated – that whatever objections might have been raised to such a scheme have already been overcome: By now the rules are in place and the situation is taken for granted – as slavery was once – by beneficiaries and victims alike.

**to confer** to give sth. such as authority, a legal right, an honour to sb.

All this is background. Ishiguro isn't much interested in the practicalities of cloning and organ donation. (Which four organs, you may wonder? A liver, two kidneys, then the heart? But wouldn't you be dead after the second kidney, anyway? Or are we throwing in the pancreas*?) Nor is this a novel about future horrors. It's set, not in a Britain yet-to-come, but in a Britain off-to-the-side, in which cloning has been introduced before the 1970s. Kathy H. is 31 in the late 1990s, which places her childhood and adolescence in the '70s and early '80s [...].

**pancreas** Bauchspeicheldrüse

Kathy H. has nothing to say about the unfairness of her fate. Indeed, she considers herself lucky to have grown up in a superior establishment like Hailsham rather than on the

standard organ farm. Like most people, she's interested in personal relationships [...]. Kathy is intelligent but not extraordinary, and she prattles on* in the obsessive manner touchy girls have, going back over past conversations and registering every comment and twitch and crush and put-down and cold shoulder and gang-up and spat*. It's all hideously* familiar and gruesomely* compelling to anyone who ever kept a teenage diary. [...]
One motif at the very core of *Never Let Me Go* is the treatment of out-groups, and the way out-groups form in-groups, even among themselves. The marginalized are not exempt from doing their own marginalization [...]. The book is also about our tendency to cannibalize others to make sure we ourselves get a soft ride [...]: The children of Hailsham are offered up on the altar of improved health for the population at large. With babies already being created with a view to their organs – help for an affected sibling, for instance – the dilemma of the Hailsham "students" is bound to become more general. Who owns your body? Who therefore is entitled to offer it up? [...]
Finally, the book is also about our wish to do well, to attract approval. The children's poignant* desire to be patted on the head – to be a good "carer," keeping those from whom organs are taken from becoming too distressed; to be a "good donor," someone who makes it through all four "donations" – is heart-breaking. This is what traps them in their cage: None of them thinks about running away or revenging themselves upon the "normal" members of society. [...]
Tellingly, two words recur again and again. One, as you might expect, is "normal." The other is "supposed," as in the last words of the book: "wherever it was that I was supposed to be going." Who defines "normal"? Who tells us what we are supposed to be doing? These questions always become more pressing in times of stress; unless I'm much mistaken, they'll loom ever larger in the next few years.
*Never Let Me Go* is unlikely to be everybody's cup of tea. The people in it aren't heroic. The ending is not comforting. Nevertheless, it is a brilliantly executed book by a master craftsman who has chosen a difficult subject: ourselves, seen through a glass, darkly.

Margaret Atwood, "Brave New World", www.slate.com, 01.04.2005 [09.01.2012]


**to prattle** to talk in a silly way for a long time about unimportant things
**spat** a short argument
**hideous** very unpleasant
**gruesome** distressing, involving or describing death or injury in a very unpleasant way

**poignant** ['pɔɪnjənt] making you feel sad, distressing to the feelings

## M 9 Physics of the Future: How Science Will Shape Human Destiny and Our Daily Lives by the Year 2100

Michio Kaku

Michio Kaku

Dr Michio Kaku is a theoretical physicist at the City University of New York and has published several books in which he explains scientific phenomena to a non-scientific audience. In his book *Physics of the Future*, published in 2011, Kaku addresses several issues from different fields of science among others also the future of medicine (from which this extract is taken), extrapolating his ideas from what is already possible today.

1. **State** the benefits Kaku sees for genetic enhancement of the human race.

2. **Explain** the author's strategy of getting his message across. Focus on his line of argument.

**3.** **Assess** Kaku's positive vision of genetic enhancement by taking possible negative side-effects into consideration.

[...] As we mentioned earlier, people often reject the advances of technology (for example, the paperless office) when it contradicts human nature, which has remained relatively constant over the past 100,000 years. People may not want to create designer children who deviate* from the norm and are considered freaks by their peers. This decreases their chances of success in society. Dressing one's children in silly clothing is one thing, but permanently changing their heredity* is an entirely different thing. (In a free market, there probably will be a place for weird genes, but it will be small, since the market will be driven by consumer demand.) More than likely, by the end of the century, a couple will be given a library of genes to choose from, mostly those for eliminating genetic diseases but also some for genetic enhancement. However, there will be little market pressure to finance the study of bizarre genes because the demand for them will be so small.
The real danger will come not so much from consumer demand but from dictatorial governments that may want to use genetic engineering for their own purposes, such as breeding stronger but more obedient soldiers.
Another problem arises in the distant future, when we have space colonies on other planets whose gravity and climatic conditions are much different from the earth's. At that point, perhaps in the next century, it becomes realistic to think of engineering a new breed of humans who can adjust to different gravity fields and atmospheric conditions. For example, a new breed of humans may be able to consume different amounts of oxygen*, adjust to a different length of day, and have a different body weight and metabolism*. But space travel will be expensive for a long time. By the end of the century, we may have a small outpost* on Mars, but an overwhelming fraction* of the human race will be on the earth. For decades to centuries to come, space travel will be for astronauts, the wealthy, and maybe a handful of hardy* space colonists.
So the splitting of the human race into different spacefaring* species around the solar system and beyond will not happen in this century, or even the next. For the foreseeable future, unless there are dramatic breakthroughs in space technology, we are largely stuck on the earth. [...]

Michio Kaku, *Physics of the Future*, Doubleday, New York 2011, pp. 194–95

**to deviate from** to vary from, to be different

**heredity** transmission of traits from parents to offspring

**oxygen** *Sauerstoff*
**metabolism** *Stoffwechsel*

**outpost** station
**fraction** part

**hardy** strong, tough
**spacefaring** space travelling

# Tyranny of Technology?

## M1 Little Brother Is Watching

Walter Kirn

This article, published on 17 October 2010 in the *New York Times*, criticises the fact that modern technology contributes to a fragmentation of society, meaning that society more and more falls apart. The article is a reaction to the suicide of Tyler Clementi, an 18-year-old student who committed suicide after he found out that he was filmed by his roommate while having a romantic interlude with another man.

1. **Point out** what the author means when he says that the invasion of privacy has been "democratized" (l. 14).
2. **Outline** how today's communication technologies and communicators differ from those Orwell imagined in his novel *1984*.
3. **State** in what way, according to the author, the actions of "Little Brother" can benefit society.
4. **Examine** how today's technology has blurred the lines between what's public and what's private.
5. **Comment** on the author's thesis that modern technology contributes to the fragmentation of society.

In George Orwell's "1984," that novel of totalitarian politics whose great mistake was to emphasize the villainy* of society's masters while playing down the mischief* of the masses, the goal of communications technology was brutal and direct: to ensure the dominance of the state. The sinister "telescreens" placed in people's homes spewed* propaganda and conducted surveillance, keeping the population passive and the leadership firmly in control. In the face of constant monitoring, all people could do was sterilize their behavior, conceal their thoughts and carry on like model citizens.

This was, it turns out, a quaint* scenario, grossly* simplistic and deeply melodramatic. As the Internet proves every day, it isn't some stern* and monolithic* Big Brother that we have to reckon with as we go about our daily lives, it's a vast cohort* of prankish* Little Brothers equipped with devices that Orwell, writing 60 years ago, never dreamed of and who are loyal to no organized authority. The invasion of privacy – of others' privacy but also our own, as we turn our lenses on ourselves in the quest for attention by any means – has been democratized.

For Tyler Clementi, the Rutgers University student who recently committed suicide after a live-stream video of an intimate encounter of his was played on the Web, Little Brother took the form of a prying* roommate with a webcam. The snoop* had no discernible* agenda other than silly, juvenile troublemaking, which made his actions more disturbing in certain ways than the oppressive prying of a dictatorship. The roommate, it seems, was acting on impulse, at least initially, and his transgression* couldn't be anticipated, let alone defended against. Clementi, unlike Orwell's Winston Smith, who hid from the telescreens whenever possible and understood that the price of personhood was ceaseless self-censorship and vigilance*, had no way of knowing that the walls

**villainy** wickedness
**mischief** harmful behaviour
**to spew** to eject, to cast forth with a lot of force
**quaint** interesting or attractive with a slightly strange and old-fashioned quality
**gross** total, extreme
**stern** strict
**monolithic** large and very powerful
**cohort** group, company
**prank** a silly trick that you play on someone to surprise them
**to pry** to be interested in someone's personal life in a way that is annoying or offensive
**snoop** sb. who tries to get secret information about sb.
**discernible** [dɪˈsɜːnəbl] clear, distinguishable
**transgression** sin, crime
**vigilance** watchfulness, caution

had eyes. Nor did his unseen observer anticipate the ultimate consequences of his intrusion*.

In "1984," the abolition of personal space was part of an overarching* government policy, but nowadays it's often nothing more than a side effect of wired high spirits. The era of the "viral video," when footage* of some absorbing slice of life can spread overnight around the globe, is bringing out the anarchist in all of us. Sometimes the results are welcome, benign*, and the intruder does his subject a favor. Take the young man who taped his girlfriend shimmying* in front of a TV attached to a Wii Fit video game. He shot the clip without her knowledge, apparently, and in no time Google and YouTube made her famous. She capitalized on* her high profile by appearing on "The Tyra Banks Show."

There are also times, of course, when Little Brother does a positive service to society by turning the tables on the state and watching the watchers. The other day a video emerged that seemed to show an Israeli soldier dancing in a mocking manner around a cowering Palestinian woman whom he appeared to have under his control. The viewer couldn't help but be reminded of more shocking pictures from Abu Ghraib* – scenes of torture that might never have come to light if Little Brother hadn't been standing nearby. The irony is that these images, which caused a convulsion* of national moral conscience, were taken – in some cases, at least – as photographic boasts or trophies. So giddy* with power and numb to its abuses were the camera-wielding prison guards that they indicted* themselves with their own antics*.

In the postideological YouTube-topia that Orwell couldn't have foreseen, information flows in all directions and does as it pleases, for better or for worse, serving no masters and obeying no party line. The telescreens, tiny, mobile and ubiquitous*, at times seem to be working independently, for some mysterious purpose all their own. This morning, when I sat down to write, I was distracted by a story on my computer about a Google Street View camera that snapped pictures of a corpse lying on a bloody street in urban Brazil. I clicked on the link, unable to do otherwise, and up came the awful, disconcerting* image. For a moment, I felt like a voyeur, spiritually dirtied by what I saw. A moment later I was checking the weather report and the status of my I.R.A.* Even Big Brother himself was not so cold. He, at least, had a motive for his peeping – to maintain order, to shore up* his position and to put down possible rebellions – but I and the countless Little Brothers like me lack any clear notion of what we're after. A fleeting sensation of omnipotence? The gratification* of idle* curiosity? Our nonstop trafficking in stolen images, sometimes as consumers and sometimes as producers (is there any meaningful difference anymore?), adds up to a story without a plot. Is it a tragic story? On occasion. It was tragic for Tyler Clementi and for his roommate, who ruined his own life by spying on another's, but for those who are suddenly lofted to fame and riches by achieving viral visibility, it's closer to a feel-good comedy.

Ours is a fragmentarian society, infinitely divided against itself and endlessly disrupted from within by much the same technologies that, in Orwell's somber* novel, assured a dull and deadening stability. In some ways, his nightmare vision of state control is cozy and reassuring by comparison. Big Brother may have stifled* dissent by forcing conformity on his frightened subjects, but his trespasses* were predictable and manageable. What's more, his assaults on citizens' privacy left the concept of privacy intact, allowing the possibility that with his overthrow people might live again as they once had.

Little Brother affords us no such luck, in part because he dwells inside us rather than in some remote and walled-off headquarters. In the new, chaotic regime of networked lenses and microphones that point every which way and rest in every hand, permitting us to train them on ourselves as easily as we aim them at one another, the private and public realms* are so confused that it's best to treat them as identical. With nowhere to hide, you

**intrusion** interference

**overarching** encompassing, overshadowing

**footage** filmed material

**benign** [bə'naɪn] kind and favourable

**to shimmy** to move your shoulders and hips from side to side as you dance or walk

**to capitalize on sth.** to make profit from sth.

**Abu Ghraib** US prison in Iraq now famous for the torture carried out there

**convulsion** outburst

**giddy** very excited and happy

**to indict** [ɪn'daɪt] to accuse sb. officially of a serious crime

**antics** (pl.) playful trick or prank, behaviour that is considered to be deliberately stupid and likely to cause problems

**ubiquitous** [juː'bɪkwɪtəs] present everywhere

**disconcerting** disturbing

**I.R.A.** Individual Retirement Account

**to shore up** to uphold, to strengthen

**gratification** fulfilment, satisfaction

**idle** insignificant, useless

**somber** gloomy, depressing

**to stifle** to prevent

**trespass** crime, wrongdoing

**realm** field, sphere

might as well perform, dispensing with old-fashioned notions of discretion and personal dignity. If Tyler Clementi had remembered to do this – to yield his personal life to the machine and acknowledge, with Shakespeare, that the world's a soundstage – he might have shrugged off* the embarrassment he suffered and made a reality show of his existence. He might have asked Little Brother into his room instead of choosing, fatally, to keep him out in the only manner he must have thought possible.

Walter Kirn, "Little Brother Is Watching", www.nytimes.com, 15.10.2010 [24.03.2014]



**to shrug off** to disregard, to minimize, to rid oneself of

## M 2 Amazon to Deliver by Drone? Don't Believe the Hype

James Ball

The online trader Amazon is looking for new ways to improve their delivery system. This article from the online service of *The Guardian*, published on 2 December 2013, sheds a critical light on the news coverage concerning the connection of logistics and military technology.

1. **State** why, according to the author, Amazon will not be able to deliver its parcels to their customers by drone in the near future.
2. **Examine** the strategy the author employs to convince his readers. Consider rhetorical devices and line of argument.
3. **Assess** the benefits and dangers of drones in our society.

@ SNG-40654-003

**paradigm** ['pærəˌdaɪm] standard
**torrent** heavy flow
**turgid** *schwülstig*
**to beleaguer** to trouble persistently, to harass
**baloney** nonsense
**BB rifle** a type of air gun
**to entail** to involve
**viable** practicable, workable
**faulty** not working, malfunctioning
**swath** *Schwade*
**et al** (Latin: et alia) and others
**clickfarm** form of click fraud, where a large group of low-paid workers is hired to click on paid advertising links for the click fraudster
**to regurgitate** to throw up

The future is here! Flying robots will, any second now, be delivering your Christmas books, DVDs and gadgets to your door within 30 minutes of you ordering them, thanks to a new initiative announced by Amazon on CBS News' 60 Minutes on Sunday.

It's a brave new world, a whole new paradigm*. Or so you'd think if you read most of the breathless coverage about the announcement, which will only get worse: expect a torrent* of turgid* think-pieces in the next 48 hours about who's going to get "disrupted" as a result of this latest shake-up – and what it means for the US's already beleaguered* postal service.

Here's the problem: it's all hot air and baloney*. As Jeff Bezos, Amazon's CEO, acknowledged in the 60 Minutes segment, his plan to begin delivery by drone won't be enacted until around 2018 – and that's a hugely optimistic timeline.

The practical issues are manifold: the technology to make the drones operational in any sense is not yet in place. It's all well and good for the unmanned vehicles to fly to a particular GPS site, but how does it then find the package's intended recipient? How is the transfer of the package enacted? What stops someone else stealing the package along the way? And what happens when next door's kid decides to shoot the drone with his BB rifle*?

None of that starts to come close to the legal minefield using drones in this way entails*. At present, flying drones of this sort for commercial use would be illegal in the US. The Federal Aviation Administration (FAA), which regulates this area, intends to make commercial drones legally viable* and workable by 2015, but this deadline is all-but impossible: managing the skies with this much low-level traffic is a problem people are nowhere near solving. Opening up crowded urban areas full of terror targets to large numbers of flying platforms is always going to be packed with conflicting interests and difficulties. And all this has come before the first lawsuit caused after someone is injured by a faulty* drone (or that one your neighbour shot), crashing down to earth.

What Jeff Bezos announced amounted, essentially, to an aspiration to change how his company delivers products, in about five years time, if technology advances and regulation falls his way. If his TV appearance hadn't included the magic word "drones", Bezos's vague aspirations to change an aspect of his company's logistics probably wouldn't have made waves. Lucky for him, he did – winning his company positive publicity just ahead of what is usually the biggest online shopping day of the year, the dreadfully named Cyber Monday.

Floating an exciting-but-impractical innovation for a swath* of press coverage is such an old PR tactic you'd hope no one would fall for it, and yet everyone still does. In an industry dominated by page views, stuff people will click on that is easy to produce is an irresistible draw. Who cares if it actually stands up?

Bezos' neat trick has knocked several real stories about Amazon out of the way. Last week's Panorama investigation into Amazon's working and hiring practices, suggesting that the site's employees had an increased risk of mental illness, is the latest in a long line of pieces about the company's working conditions – zero-hour contracts, short breaks, and employees' every move tracked by internal systems. Amazon's drone debacle also moved discussion of its tax bill – another long-running controversy, sparked by the Guardian's revelation last year that the company had UK sales of £7bn but paid no UK corporation tax – to the margins. The technology giants – Amazon, Google, Microsoft et al* – have huge direct reach to audiences and customers, the money to hire swarms of PR and communications staff, and a technology press overwhelmingly happy to incredulously print almost every word, rather than to engage in the much harder task of actually holding them to account.

It's too late for the clickfarms* already. But outlets and journalists who'd like to think of themselves as serious must stop regurgitating* this crap. And, even more importantly, you, concerned citizen, must try to stop clicking on it.

James Ball, "Amazon to deliver by drone? Don't believe the hype", www.theguardian.com, 02.12.2013 [15.02.2014]

## M 3 Wearable Technology

The following three latest innovative technologies can be characterised as "wearable technology" or "wearable tech", meaning that technical devices can be worn as clothes or accessories thus extending the possibilities of the human senses.

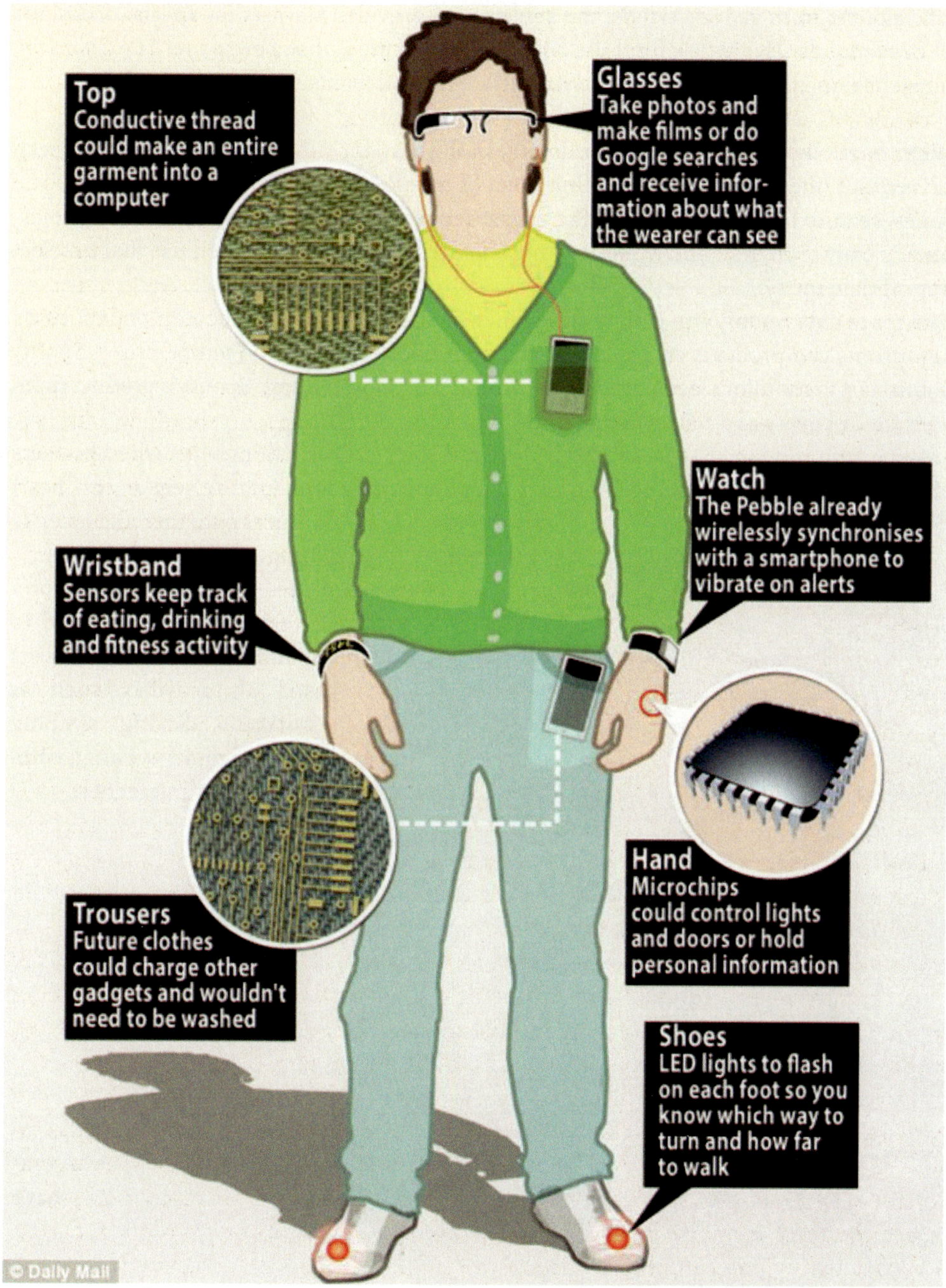


Work in small groups. Choose one of the articles and find out about advantages and disadvantages of the respective new technology. Be prepared to present your results.

# M 3a Spotify to Tailor Music to Your Heart Beat

Samuel Gibbs

The music service *Spotify* provides its customers with a free online music stream featuring music from artists under contract with the large music labels. Apart from listening to specific albums from various artists, the service also provides playlists for special occasions or even moods. This article from the online service of the British newspaper *The Guardian*, published on 20 January 2014, presents the latest trend in customising the service.

What might be the perfect tune for dozing in the sun, for running along a stormy beach or, perhaps, the soundtrack to the first flush of true love?

A new feature being discussed by the music service Spotify could use sensors on the listener's body or in their smartphone to measure their heart rate and then use that to select appropriate music.

The more data Spotify can collect on listener habits, the better the recommendations its algorithms can produce. As well as music, motion, heart rate, and temperature, Spotify could start to monitor sleep patterns, according to Donovan Sung, Spotify's product manager for discovery and recommendations.

"Maybe with motion sensors in phones, we can start guessing things like whether users are running, biking or driving? Maybe if the phone has a temperature sensor, or a heart rate sensor, we could guess whether the user is tense* ..." said Sung, talking to TechRadar.

**tense** under stress, pressure

Sung explained that information provided by sensors could be used to automatically generate playlists based on activities such as workouts, driving, sleeping or late-night working, without user interaction.

The service could automatically start playing pumping music when it is time to go for a run or peaceful ambient tracks for when sleep is required.

"The more we know about you, the better the [recommendation] engine can be," said Sung, who warned that overloading listeners with choice provided a poor user experience, and that a fine balance must be struck between quantity and quality of recommendations.

**Human editors, algorithms and social data**

Spotify's recommendation engine is currently powered by a combination of human editors, algorithms, social data and previous listening history, which provide personal recommendations for users of artists, albums and tracks. These also inform Spotify's shuffle play feature, which it unveiled* in December 2013 and is continuing to improve.

"Nearly half of mobile listening, if not more, is people listening to their own curated* playlists," said Daniel Ek, Spotify's founder at the time. "With shuffle play, you can now play any of your playlists for free. Spotify's new mobile experience is music for anyone and the best experience and access in the history of music."

Samuel Gibbs, "Spotify to tailor music to your heart beat", www.theguardian.com, 20.01.2014 [24.03.2014]

**to unveil** to reveal, to disclose
**to curate** here: to select

## M3b Sense and Sensorbility: The Book That Lets You Feel Your Protagonist's Pain

Alison Flood

This article from the online service of the British newspaper *The Guardian* from 28 January 2014 presents a wearable book that opens a totally new dimension of reading and empathy.

It's straight out of the pages of science fiction: a "wearable" book, which uses temperature controls and lighting to mimic the experiences of a story's protagonist, has been dreamed up by academics at MIT*.

The book, explain the researchers, senses the page a reader is on, and changes ambient lighting and vibrations to "match the mood". A series of straps form a vest which contains a "heartbeat and shiver* simulator", a body compression system, temperature controls and sound.

"Changes in the protagonist's emotional or physical state trigger discrete feedback in the wearable [vest], whether by changing the heartbeat rate, creating constriction through air pressure bags, or causing localised temperature fluctuations," say the academics.

Dubbed "sensory fiction", the idea was developed by Felix Heibeck, Alexis Hope and Julie Legault at MIT's media lab. The prototype story used was James Tiptree Jr's Hugo award-winning novella *The Girl Who Was Plugged In*, in which the protagonist P Burke – who is deformed by pituitary dystrophy* and herself experiences life through an avatar – feels "both deep love and ultimate despair, the freedom of Barcelona sunshine and the captivity of a dark damp cellar", said the researchers.

"Sensory fiction is about new ways of experiencing and creating stories," they write. "Traditionally, fiction creates and induces emotions and empathy through words and images. By using a combination of networked sensors and actuators*, the sensory fiction author is provided with new means of conveying plot, mood, and emotion while still allowing space for the reader's imagination. These tools can be wielded* to create an immersive* storytelling experience tailored to the reader.

"To explore this idea, we created a connected book and wearable [vest]. The 'augmented'

**MIT** The Massachusetts Institute of Technology, a private research university in the US
**shiver** *Zittern*

**pituitary dystrophy** *Mangel an Wachstumshormonen*

**actuator** a kind of motor

**to wield** to use
**immersive** involving

book portrays the scenery and sets the mood, and the wearable allows the reader to experience the protagonist's physiological emotions."

A video shows the device in action – although what happens to the reader when P Burke meets her miserable end was not elaborated upon. A "monument to pituitary dystrophy. No surgeon would touch her", Tiptree's creation P Burke becomes a "Remote", operating the body of the beautiful Delphi and living a life through her. When she, through Delphi, falls in love with Paul, things don't end well:

*It's really P Burke five thousand miles away who loves Paul. P Burke the monster, down in a dungeon, smelling of electrode-paste. A caricature of a woman burning, melting, obsessed with true love. Trying over twenty-double-thousand miles of hard vacuum to reach her beloved through the girl-flesh numbed by an invisible film. Feeling his arms around the body he thinks is hers, fighting through shadows to give herself to him. Trying to taste and smell him through beautiful dead nostrils, to love him back with a body that goes dead in the heart of the fire ... Perhaps you get P Burke's state of mind?*

The Arthur C Clarke award-winning science fiction novelist Chris Beckett wrote about a similar invention in his novel *Marcher*, although his "sensory" experience comes in the form of a video game:

*In the spare bedroom on the first floor a group of young men were gathered around a TV. They were all plugged into a device called a dreamer, very popular in that world, though unknown in this, and were playing the classic dreamer game called Ripper Killer. They had on 3D goggles and wore things called moodpads on their heads which gave low-voltage jolts* to the hypothalamus* in order to induce elation*, longing or (as was famously the case with Ripper Killer) terror.*

**jolt** here: impulse
**hypothalamus** a part of the brain
**elation** great happiness

Adam Roberts, another prize-winning science fiction writer, found the idea of "sensory" fiction "amazing", but also "infantalising, like reverting to those sorts of books we buy for toddlers* that have buttons in them to generate relevant sound-effects".

**toddlers** children

"Books affect our minds; that's the sort of machines books are. The urge to make the books directly affect our bodies as well is a sort of category error. A massage, or a fairground ride, or the sort of rock concert where there are so many speakers you feel every chord vibrating through your chest: they're all fine. But they aren't offering the sorts of pleasures that are uniquely bookish," said Roberts.

"Emotions that start in the head and move into the body are far more effective than faux-emotional responses mimicked by flashing lights and pressure pads."

Alison Flood, "Sense and sensorbility: the book that lets you feel your protagonist's pain", www.theguardian.com, 28.01.2014 [15.02.2014]

## M 3c Child-Tracking Wristbands Edge Us Closer to a Dystopian Future

Rory Carroll

Journalist Rory Carroll writes critically about a new device which makes it easier for parents to control every move of their children. The article was published on 10 January 2014 on the website of the online service of the British newspaper *The Guardian*.

For those who think the NSA the worst invader of privacy, I invite you to share an afternoon with Aiden and Foster, two 11-year-old boys, as they wrap up* a Friday at school. Aiden invites his friend home to hang out and they text their parents, who agree to the plan.

**to wrap up** to finish

As they ride on the bus Foster's phone and a sensor on a wristband alert the school and his parents of a deviation* from his normal route. The school has been notified that he is heading to Aiden's house so the police are not called.

As they enter the house, the integrated home network recognises Aiden and pings* an advisory to his parents, both out at work, who receive the messages on phones and tablets. The system also sends Foster's data – physical description, address, relatives, health indicators, social media profile – to Aiden's parents, who note he has a laptop. Might the boys visit unsuitable sites? No, because Foster's parental rating access, according to his profile, is limited to PG13, as is Aiden's.

Foster spots a cookie jar and reaches in. Beep beep! His wristband vibrates to warn him the cookies contain gluten, and he is allergic.

Aiden's mother notes this and consults a menu of her fridge and pantry*, all connected to the network, for non-gluten ingredients. There aren't enough so she orders a gluten-free pizza.

The boys turn on the TV. Rather, it turns itself on as Aiden approaches and it lists his favourite channels. The TV notes the boys have a basketball, which has a sensor, and so suggests an NBA game. As they watch, tailored* advertising invites Aiden to put a Miami Heat shirt on a personal wishlist connected to a chain store. He does so and a ping is sent to his mother, who simultaneously receives a reminder of the date of his birthday.

The network notes there is only 90 minutes left of sunlight left and that Aiden has not completed his 120 minutes of daily exercise. It shuts down the TV and gives the boys three exercise options. They choose to shoot hoops* in the yard. Aiden's mum receives an alert that they have left the house – leaving the lights on. She can track Aiden's pulse and blood pressure as he plays.

Welcome to the future of parenting, as envisaged by Cisco Systems at the Consumer Electronics Show in Las Vegas this week. Robert Barlow, a marketing executive, presented the scenario with animation, graphs and statistics to industry professionals.

"The technology for all this already exists," he beamed*, holding a real basketball with a sensor. Cisco can aggregate* data from multiple sources to create an "orchestration layer", he said, which will help the Internet of Everything generate trillions of dollars in the next decade. [...]

What of Aiden and Foster? You could say, lucky them. Protected from predators and pornography, nudged away* from harmful food and obesity, the benefits are obvious.

I say, God help them. What sort of childhood is it with every move tracked, scrutinised*, logged*, judged? Where you cannot wander, try something new, be spontaneous – be yourself – without issuing a beeping alert from wearable, connected technology? This is helicopter parenting at its most stultifying*, a constant, hovering presence. [...]

Rory Carroll, "Child-tracking wristbands edge us closer to a dystopian future", www.theguardian.com, 10.01.2014 [15.02.2014]

**deviation** change, alteration

**to ping** here: to send a message

**pantry** kitchen storage room

**to tailor** to adjust, to make to fit

**to shoot hoops** to play basketball

**to beam** to smile broadly

**to aggregate** to combine into a collection

**to nudge** to bump, to elbow

**to scrutinise** to examine closely

**to log** to record

**to stultify** to cause to appear absurd

# M4 Surrogates and Avatars

Michio Kaku

In this extract from his book *Physics of the Future*, published in 2011, theoretical physicist Michio Kaku elaborates on the future of the scientific field of robotics and its benefits for humanity.

1. The first picture provided is called "The Creation of Adam" and is perhaps the most famous part of Michelangelo's fresco covering the ceiling of the Sistine Chapel in the Vatican. It depicts the very moment in which God breathes life into Adam. Against the backdrop of this information, come up with an explanation of the meaning and possible implications of the second picture.
2. **State** the difference between "surrogates" and "avatars" and **describe** their possible future application.
3. **Illustrate** how robots might be used in dangerous environments and **explain** their benefits compared to humans.
4. **Interpret** the expression "mind over matter" (l. 25) as used by Kaku.
5. **Discuss** positive and negative implications of the notion "mind over matter", based on your results from task 4.

Michelangelo: The Creation of Adam

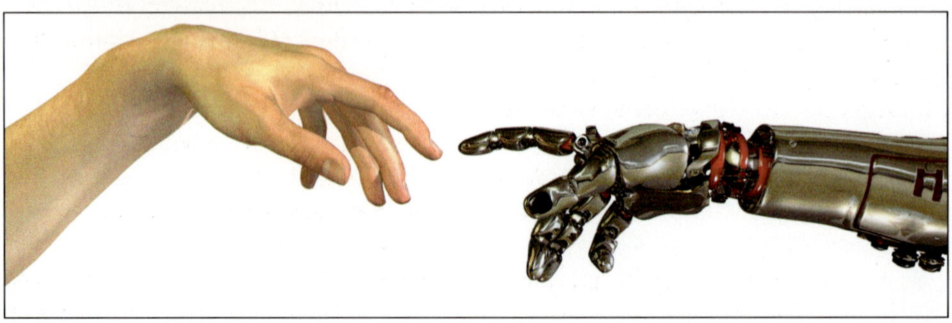

Jake Sully (Sam Worthington) and his avatar

One way in which to merge with robots, but without altering the human body, is to create surrogates or avatars. In the movie *Surrogates*, starring Bruce Willis, in the year 2017 scientists have discovered a way for people to control robots as if they were inside them, so that we can live our lives in perfect bodies. The robot responds to every command, and the person also sees and feels everything the robot sees and feels. While our mortal bodies decay and wither*, we can control the motions of our robot surrogate, which has superhuman powers and is perfectly shaped. The movie gets complicated because people prefer to live out their lives as beautiful, handsome, and superpowerful robots, abandoning* their rotting bodies, which are conveniently* hidden away. The entire human race, in effect, willingly becomes robotic rather than face reality.

In the movie *Avatar*, this is taken one step further. Instead of living our lives as perfect robots, in the year 2154 we might be able to live as alien beings. In the movie, our bodies are placed in pods*, which then allow us to control the motion of specially cloned alien bodies. In a sense, we are given entirely new bodies to live on a new planet. In this way, we can better communicate with a native alien population on other planets. The movie plot thickens when one worker decides to abandon his humanity and live out his life as an alien, protecting them from mercenaries*.

These surrogates and avatars are not possible today but may be possible in the future. Recently, ASIMO* has been programmed with a new idea: remote sensing*. At Kyoto University, humans have been trained to control the mechanical motion of robots by using brain sensors. For example, by putting on an EEG helmet, students can move the arms and legs of ASIMO by simply thinking. So far, four distinct motions of the arms and head are possible. This may open the door to another realm* of AI*: robots controlled by the mind.

Although this is a crude* demonstration of mind over matter, in the coming decades it should be possible to increase the set of motions we can control in a robot, and also to get feedbacks, so we can "feel" with our new robotic hands. Goggles* or contact lenses would allow us to see what the robots see, so we might eventually have full control over the body's motions.

This may also help alleviate the immigration problem for Japan. Workers may be located in different countries, yet control robots thousands of miles away by donning* brain sen-

**to wither** to fade

**to abandon** to leave behind
**convenient** comfortably, simply

**pod** capsule

**mercenary** person who fights, kills for money

**ASIMO** (Advanced Step in Innovative Mobility) a humanoid robot able to walk on two legs
**remote sensing** acquisition of information about an object or phenomenon without making physical contact with the object
**realm** [rɛlm] domain, field
**AI** abbreviation for Artificial Intelligence
**crude** simple
**goggles** glasses
**to don** to wear

**white-collar worker** person who performs professional, managerial, or administrative work
**blue-collar worker** a working class person who performs manual labour
**to grapple with** to deal with, to cope with

**application** use

**high-voltage line** power line

**hazardous** dangerous, unpredictable

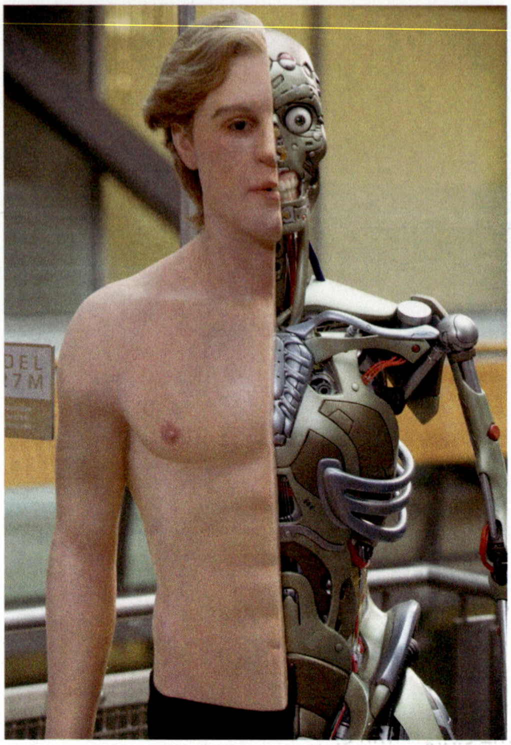

Half-human, half-robot from the film *Surrogates*

sors. So not only can the Internet carry the thoughts of white-collar workers*, it might also carry the thoughts of blue-collar workers* and translate them into physical motion. This might mean that robots will become an integral part of any nation grappling* with exploding health costs and a shortage of workers.
Controlling robots by remote sensing may also have applications* elsewhere. In any dangerous environment (for example, underwater, near high-voltage lines*, in fires), robots controlled by human thoughts may be used in rescue missions. Or undersea robots may be connected directly to humans, so that humans can control many swimming robots by thoughts alone. Since the surrogate would have superpowers, it would be able to chase criminals (unless the criminals also have superpowered surrogates). One would have all the advantages of merging with robots without changing our bodies at all.
Such an arrangement might actually prove useful for space exploration, when we have to manage a permanent moon base. Our surrogates may perform all the dangerous tasks of maintaining the moon base, while the astronauts are safely back on earth. The astronauts would use the superstrength and the superpowers of the robots while exploring a hazardous* alien landscape. (This would not work if the astronauts are on the earth controlling surrogates on Mars, however, since radio signals take up to 40 minutes to go from the earth to Mars and back. But it would work if the astronauts were sitting safely in a permanent base on Mars while the surrogates went out and performed dangerous tasks on the Martian surface.

Michio Kaku, *Physics of the Future*, Doubleday, New York 2011, pp. 128–130

## M5 A Day in Life in 2100

Michio Kaku

In this extract from his book *The Physics of the Future*, theoretical physicist Michio Kaku talks about a typical day in the life of a man in the year 2100. This extract focuses on what happens when John, a fictitious person, comes home from work.

1. Make a list of all the futuristic elements which occur in the text, then **describe** them in detail.

2. **Compare** John's leisure time with your own.

**3.** Obviously, John prefers having his co-workers over to watch football rather than their holographic images. What does this tell you about the future of human interaction and sociability? **Justify** your opinion.

**4.** Imagine time travel was possible. As a reporter, you travel into the year 2100 and meet John. After having spent the evening together, you travel back and write a newspaper article about your experience in the future. The headline of your article is "A Day in 2100 – does technology dictate human life?"

## Home Again

[...] You finally arrive back home again. You are exhausted. Just as you sink comfortably into your sofa, Molly appears on the wall screen. "John, you have an important message from Dr. Brown."

Dr. Brown? What does your robot doctor have to say?

"Put him on screen," you say to Molly. Your doctor appears on the wall screen. "Dr. Brown" is so realistic that you sometimes forget that he is just a software program.

"Sorry to bother you, John, but there is something I have to bring to your attention. Remember your skiing accident last year, the one that almost killed you?"

How could you forget? You still cringe* when you remember how you plowed* into a tree while skiing in what is left of the Alps. Since most of the Alpine snow has already melted, you had to choose an unfamiliar resort at a very high altitude*. Unaccustomed to* the territory, you accidentally tumbled down the slope* and slammed into a bunch of trees at 40 miles per hour. Ouch!

Dr. Brown continues, "My records show that you were knocked unconscious, suffering a concussion* and massive internal injuries, but your clothes saved your life."

Although you were unconscious, your clothes automatically called for an ambulance, uploaded your medical history, and located your precise coordinates. Then at the hospital robots performed microsurgery* to stop the bleeding, sew up tiny ruptured* blood vessels*, and patch up* other damage.

"Your stomach, liver, and intestines* were damaged beyond repair," Dr. Brown reminds you. "Luckily, we could grow a new set of organs for you just in time."

Suddenly, you feel a little bit like a robot yourself, with so much of your body made from organs grown in a tissue* factory.

"You know, John, my records also show that you could have replaced your shattered arm with a fully mechanical one. The latest robot arm would have increased the strength in your arm by a factor of five. But you declined*."

"Yes," you reply, "I guess I'm still an old-fashioned guy. I'll take flesh over steel any day," you say.

"John, we have to do a periodic* checkup on your new organs. Pick up your MRI scanner and slowly pass it over your stomach area."

You go to the bathroom and pick up a small device, about the size of cell phone, and slowly pass it over your organs. Immediately on the wall screen, you can see the 3-D image of your internal organs lighting up.

"John, we are going to analyze these images to see how your body is healing. By the way, this morning the DNA sensors in your bathroom detected cancer growing in your pancreas*."

"Cancer?" You suddenly straighten up. You are puzzled. "But I thought cancer was cured years ago. No one even talks about it much anymore. How can I have cancer?"

"Actually, scientists never cured cancer. Let's just say that we are in a truce* with cancer, a stalemate*. There are too many kinds of cancer. Like a common cold. We never cured

**to cringe** to tremble, to shiver
**to plow into** to collide, to crash
**altitude** height
**unaccustomed to** unfamiliar with
**slope** *Abhang*
**concussion** *Gehirnerschütterung*

**microsurgery** surgery requiring an operating microscope
**to rupture** to break open
**blood vessel** *Blutgefäße*
**to patch up** to repair
**intestines** *Eingeweide*
**tissue** *Gewebe*

**to decline** to refuse

**periodic** regular

**pancreas** *Bauchspeicheldrüse*

**truce** peaceful solution
**stalemate** deadlock, standstill

**to keep sth. at bay** to prevent sth. from harming you
**to zap** to destroy
**to deadpan** to display no personal envolvement
**relief** comfort

that, either. We simply keep it at bay*. I've ordered some nanoparticles to zap* those cancer cells. There are only a few hundred of them. Just routine. But without this intervention, you would probably die in about seven years," he deadpans*.

"Oh, that's a relief*," you say to yourself.

"Yes, today we can spot cancer years before a tumor forms," says Dr. Brown.

"Tumor? What's that?"

"Oh, that's an old-fashioned word for a type of advanced cancer. It's pretty much disappeared from the language. We never see them anymore," adds Dr. Brown.

Then you realize that in all this excitement, you forgot that your sister threatened to set you up with someone. You call up Molly again.

"Molly, I am not doing anything this weekend, so can you find a date for me? You know the kind of person I like."

**to display** to show

"Yes, your preferences are programmed in my memory. Wait a minute while I scan the Internet." After a minute, Molly displays* the profiles of promising candidates who are also sitting in front of their wall screens, asking the same questions.

**to appeal to sb.** to catch sb.'s eye

After scanning the candidates, you finally select one who appeals to* you. This person, called Karen, somehow looks special, you think to yourself. "Molly, send Karen a polite message, asking her if she is available this weekend. There's a new restaurant that just opened that I want to try."

Molly sends Karen your profile in a video mail.

**caveman** *Höhlenmensch*
**to bond with sb.** to connect, to bind

That night, you relax by having some of your coworkers come over for beer and to watch some football. Your friends could have watched the game by appearing in your living room via holographic images, but somehow, cheering for the home team is more enjoyable with your friends joining in the excitement in person. You smile, imagining that this is probably how it was thousands of years ago, when cavemen* had to bond with* one another.

Suddenly, the entire living room is illuminated, and it appears as if you are right on the football field, at the 50-yard line. As the game is being played all around you.

**to size up** to assess sb. or sth.

During halftime, you and your friends begin sizing up* the players. Over beer, popcorn, you hotly debate who trains the most, practices the hardest, has the best coaches, and has the best gene therapist. Your home team, you all agree, has the best geneticist in the league, with the best genes that money can buy.

After your friends have left, you still are too excited to go to sleep. So you decide to play a quick game of poker before turning in.

"Molly," you ask, "it's late, but I want to set up a game of poker. I'm feeling lucky. Someone must be awake in England, China, India, or Russia who might want to play a few hands right now."

**to relish** to appreciate

"No problem," says Molly. A number of promising faces appear on the screen. As the 3-D images of each player materialize in your living room, you relish* the idea of seeing who can bluff the best. It's funny, you say to yourself that you are more familiar with people in distant countries, thousands of miles away, than with your next-door neighbors. National boundaries don't mean much these days.

Finally, just before you finally turn in, Molly interrupts you again, appearing in the bathroom mirror.

**to verify** to prove
**accuracy** correctness

"John, Karen accepted your invitation. Everything is set for this weekend. I will make a reservation at that new restaurant. Do you want to see the profile that she wrote about herself? Do you want me to scan the Internet to verify* the accuracy* of her profile? People have been known to ... ah ... lie about their profiles."

"No," you say. "Let's keep it a surprise for the weekend." After that poker game, you feel lucky again.

Michio Kaku, *Physics of the Future*, Doubleday, New York 2011, pp. 414–417

# Are We All Friends Now?
# Boon and Bane of Social Media

## M1 The Meaningful Irrelevance of Being Connected!?

The picture below is a Facebook "map of the world" created by Paul Butler, an intern on Facebook's data infrastructure engineering team. He wanted to see if geographical and political borders affected friendships as well as which cities had the most social connections. He started by using a sample of ten million friend pairs, correlated them with their current cities and then mapped that data using the longitude and latitude of each city. The result is "not just a pretty picture, it's a reaffirmation of the impact we have in connecting people, even across oceans and borders" (Butler).

1. **Describe** what the visualisation of the Facebook network tells you about the various connections.

2. Facebook is the largest social network, with over 1 billion active users, many of whom have more than 100 friends within the network. With this in mind, **comment** on the statement in the headline of **M1**.

**ZOOM IN: Terminology**

In contrast to traditional media, the term **social media** refers to the collective of online communications channels dedicated to community-based input, interaction, content-sharing and collaboration. Among the different types of social media are mainly websites and applications dedicated to forums, (micro)blogging, social bookmarking, wikis, instant messaging and social networking. Social media are therefore tools for sharing and discussing information whereas social networking is rather the collaboration and interaction of communities of interest. The most prominent examples of social media in general are Facebook, Wikipedia, Twitter, reddit, LinkedIn, YouTube, Instagram.
**Traditional media** are means of communication and expression that have been established before the advent of the Internet. They include print publications, broadcast and cable television, radio, film and music. The main differences between traditional and new or social media are the direction of communication and the time it takes to transmit information. Traditional media communication is usually considered to be slower and cannot engage in social discourse as easily as social media is able to.

## M 2a Social Networking: A Social 'Eden' or Dystopian Tool?

Olivia Aldridge

In the following comment on social networking, published in October 2013 in *The Red & Black*, an independent student newspaper serving the University of Georgia, the author questions the positive implications of befriending people online and sharing private information that way.

1. Draw a table depicting positive and negative aspects of social networks. Write down at least three arguments in each column. Exchange your results with your partner.

2. **Point out** which further positive and negative arguments are provided in the text. Add them to your list from task 1.

3. Several times Aldridge refers to George Orwell's novel *1984*. With regard to the excerpt from *1984* in **M 2b**, **explain** why, according to Aldridge, it is logical that "social media is progressing us towards Orwell's classic dystopian novel". Pay special attention to the role of language.

4. Against the backdrop of your findings from the tasks above, **discuss** whether social networks like Facebook are a social 'Eden' or a dystopian tool.

The summer after eighth grade, I secretly created a Facebook account at my best friend's house. It didn't take me long to admit this to my mother, who rather than order me to delete it, told me to read "1984" by George Orwell. I nodded, I said I might and I didn't. But she continued to warn me about the dangers of putting personal information and thoughts online, and often repeated her instruction to read the book, saying that if I did, I would rethink social media.

Flash forward to the tail end of my junior year of high school. Mr. Patrick, my American Lit[erature] teacher, prescribed me with some reading direction. When he lent me his personal copy of "1984," I didn't really have a choice. So the first week of summer, when it was nap time at my babysitting gig*, I finally read the book.

Even those who haven't read Orwell's classic dystopian novel are probably familiar with many of its central themes. Many of Orwell's "1984" based expressions have seeped into regular conversation – the concept of "Big Brother" was born out of "1984", as was "doublethink," "newspeak" and "the thought police."

Now having read the book, I can see my mom's point. The argument that social media is progressing us towards Orwell's dystopia is logical in some ways. Certainly we are more careless with our privacy. We know that posting our contact info, opinions, life events and photos can leave a lasting online fingerprint, and yet social media has become so deeply ingrained* in our lives that we throw caution to the wind.

Social media is becoming more and more personal. When we post on Facebook from our phones, our location appears at the bottom of a post. Any location we are "tagged" in is collected into a detailed map of lives. The advertisements on the side of the page change based on what we "like" and which ads we click on. Social media websites seem to be increasingly able to delve into our personalities and tastes.

So if social media is watching us, is Big Brother watching us, too? The Snowden scandal made it clear that government-based Internet surveillance is real, after all.

But I'll drop pretenses* of conspiracy theorizing. True, social media makes us easier to watch. But the very nature of social media is the voluntary* sharing of information. The modern individual has two personas: their physical, real life persona and their online persona. Social media users project themselves as they want to be seen. They sculpt* their profiles to represent a character, and this is what keeps them safe from an Orwellian dystopia. The intelligent users control what aspects of their life and personality are available.

In "1984," Orwell describes many futuristic technologies that proved to be self-fulfilling prophecies – telescreens for example, resemble the Skype of today. What Orwell didn't imagine was that his technologies would be popularized as open-forum and consumerist creations. Social media changed the whole game, giving people voices rather than stifling* them like Big Brother did.

Numerous social and political movements have been enabled by social media. From Arab Spring uprisings to marriage equality, social media users have generated social and political awareness through what they post, share, "like" and retweet. Government surveillance can't change the fact that social media is by the people, for the people.

My mom's generation is intimidated by the rapid societal changes social media brings, and perhaps social media does have dangerous side effects. But despite many resemblances to Orwell's imagined future, a Big-Brother censored dystopia isn't one of them.

Olivia Aldridge, "Dystopian Days: '1984' and now", www.redandblack.com, 11.10.2013 [01.02.2014]

**gig** here: job

**ingrained** *verwurzelt*

**pretense** *Vortäuschung*

**voluntary** *freiwillig*

**to sculpt** *formen*

**to stifle** *unterdrücken, abwürgen*

# M2b Nineteen Eighty-Four

## George Orwell

Eric Arthur Blair (1903–1950), known by his pen name George Orwell, was an English author and journalist. In his works he was focused on raising awareness of social injustice and fighting totalitarianism. He is best known for his satirical novella *Animal Farm* (1945) and the dystopian novel *1984*, originally published in 1949.

The novel *1984* depicts the superstate Oceania, a totalitarian dictatorship under the rule of Big Brother. Living conditions for the masses are poor as Oceania is a world of constant war, omnipresent government surveillance, and public mind control, dictated by a political system euphemistically named English Socialism ("Ingsoc"). The protagonist, Winston Smith, is a civil servant in the Ministry of Truth (Newspeak: "Minitrue"). He is responsible for keeping alive the Party's propaganda by changing historical records. Winston secretly hates the Party and eventually rebels against Big Brother. Among the various instruments of control the Party applies, there is the fictional language of Newspeak. The following excerpt shows its function and how it works.

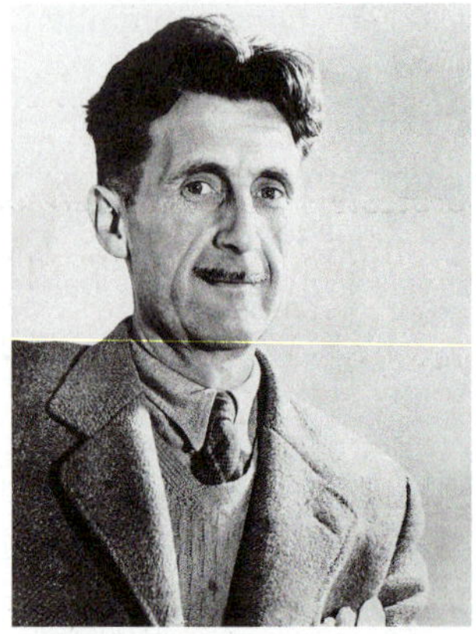

George Orwell working for the BBC between 1941–1943

"It's a beautiful thing, the Destruction of words. Of course the great wastage* is in the verbs and adjectives, but there are hundreds of nouns that can be got rid of as well. It isn't only the synonyms; there are also the antonyms. After all, what justification is there for a word, which is simply the opposite of some other word? A word contains its opposite in itself. Take 'good,' for instance. If you have a word like 'good,' what need is there for a word like 'bad'? 'Ungood' will do just as well – better, because it's an exact opposite, which the other is not. Or again, if you want a stronger version of 'good,' what sense is there in having a whole string of vague useless words like 'excellent' and 'splendid' and all the rest of them? 'Plusgood' covers the meaning or 'doubleplusgood' if you want something stronger still. Of course we use those forms already, but in the final version of Newspeak there'll be nothing else. In the end the whole notion of goodness and badness will be covered by only six words – in reality, only one word. Don't you see the beauty of that, Winston? It was B.B.'s* idea originally, of course," he added as an afterthought. [...]

"Don't you see that the whole aim of Newspeak is to narrow the range of thought? In the end we shall make thoughtcrime* literally impossible, because there will be no words in which to express it. Every concept that can ever be needed will be expressed by exactly one word, with its meaning rigidly defined and all its subsidiary meanings rubbed out and forgotten."

George Orwell, *Nineteen Eighty-Four*, Penguin, London 2008, p. 54 f.

**wastage** waste

**B.B.** Big Brother

**thoughtcrime** the criminal act of harbouring a thought or belief against the ruling party

# M3 Revolution 2.0 – Social Media Sparked Egypt's Revolutionary Fire

Sam Gustin

The Egyptian Revolution of 2011 was a diverse movement of demonstrations, marches, plaza occupations, riots and violent clashes with the security forces, where millions of protesters from a variety of socio-economic and religious backgrounds demanded the overthrow of the regime of Egyptian President Hosni Mubarak. After 18 days of fierce protests, Mubarak announced he was stepping down on February 12, 2011, bringing to an end his 30-year regime. In his article from November 2011, Sam Gustin reviews the influence and impact social media had on this conflict.

1. In keywords, collect as many forms and types of communication and media as possible (e.g. pictures, books). Together with a partner evaluate which type of communication can reach the largest audience, which type is most appealing, which is most manipulative, which transports the biggest amount of information.

2. **Describe** the function of social media in Egypt's Revolution as presented in the article.

3. Wael Ghonim praises Facebook as an inspiration and major support for the revolution. He humorously states that Facebook knows where the next revolution is going to take place implying that social media will be of importance again. **Evaluate** the role of social networks in the context of such a revolution.

Activists in Tahrir Square in Cairo, Egypt

**repression** *Unterdrückung*
**despotic rule** tyrannic rule
**kindling** wood to start a fire with
**accelerant** *Brandbeschleuniger*
**to galvanize** to stimulate

If three decades of violent repression* and despotic rule* were kindling* for the Egyptian revolution, social media was both a spark and an accelerant* for the movement.

Did social media like Facebook and Twitter cause the revolution? No. But these tools did speed up the process by helping to organize the revolutionaries, transmit their message to the world and galvanize* international support.

"In the same way that pamphlets didn't cause the American Revolution, social media didn't cause the Egyptian revolution," said Sascha Meinrath, director of the New America Foundation's Open Technology Initiative. "Social media have become the pamphlets of the 21st century, a way that people who are frustrated with the status quo can organize themselves and coordinate protest, and in the case of Egypt, revolution."

**truism** *Binsenweisheit*

It is a truism* in political science that successful revolutions are born in the streets – from the Boston Massacre of March 1770 and the storming of the Bastille in Paris in July 1789, to the streets of Cairo in January and February 2011. What has shocked most observers of the current Egyptian scene is the sheer speed with which the regime fell – 18 days.

And that's where modern communications technology has had the most potent impact. Rafat Ali, a social media expert and founder of PaidContent, said Facebook and Twitter played different roles in the uprising. Facebook helped to organize the activists inside the country, he said, while Twitter functioned to help get the message out to the broader world.

"Facebook definitely had a role in organizing this revolution," Ali told Wired.com. "It acts like an accelerant to conditions which already exist in the country. Twitter and YouTube serve as amplification for what's happening on the ground. And they directly affect Western media coverage."

"One of the things that social media does is transmission of hope across these countries," Ali added, referring to Tunisia, Egypt and other repressed countries in the Middle East.

Ali said the regimes in Tunisia and Egypt had underestimated the power of technology to organize activists and drive the movement.

"These despots are five generations older than the youth," Ali said. "None of these people in their 60s, 70s, and 80s have ever used Facebook or Twitter."

Lawrence Pintak, author of *The New Arab Journalist*, pointed out on CNN that despite the speed with which the Mubarak regime fell, bloggers and digital activists have been working toward reform under violent repression in the Middle East for years. "This is a digital revolution that has been happening for quite a while," Pintak said.

**to catalyze** to link

CNN host Anderson Cooper earlier asked former CIA director James Woolsey whether the U.S. intelligence community has fully grasped the power of social media in catalyzing* pro-democracy movements worldwide.

"I think they're starting to," Woolsey replied. "I know people who for years now have been trying to get them to help get the right types of equipment and software into places like Iran in order to take advantage of people's desire for freedom."

"We should have been doing exactly what has happened in Egypt," Woolsey added. "We should have been trying to help foster* that in Iran, helping them set up servers to protect their Facebooks, protect their Twitters, and we really have not."

Wael Ghonim, the young Google executive who has become a symbol of Egypt's pro-democracy uprising after he launched* the original Facebook page credited with sparking the initial protest, called the Egyptian upheaval*, "Revolution 2.0." "If you want to liberate a country, give them the Internet," Ghonim said.

He credited Facebook and its young founder Mark Zuckerberg as an inspiration.

"This revolution started on Facebook," Ghonim told CNN. "I want to meet Mark Zuckerberg some day and thank him personally."

Asked by CNN host Wolf Blitzer what repressive Middle Eastern state would be the next to fall, the young activist replied: "Ask Facebook."

Sam Gustin, "Social Media Sparked, Accelerated Egypt's Revolutionary Fire", www.wired.com, 02.11.2011 [01.02.2014]

**to foster** to support, to back up

**to launch** to start

**upheaval** overthrow

Do further research on the Arab Spring, the revolutionary wave of protests, riots and civil wars in the Arab World which started in December 2010. Pay special attention to the importance of social media and digital technology as a means of collective activism. Present your results in class.
Research tip: Inside the Egyptian revolution

@ SNG-40654-004

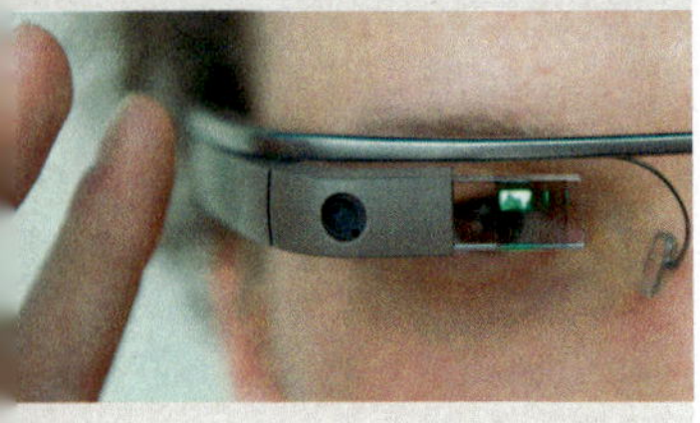

# M 4 The Dystopian Future of Google Glass

Adam L. Penenberg

In his article, published in 2013, Penenberg envisions the future social experience of augmented reality (see "Terminology", p. 68) using Google's Glass technology. Google Glass is a wearable computer with an optical head-mounted display. It shows information in a smartphone-like hands-free format, and can communicate with the Internet via language voice commands.

1. Think about today's way of social and technological communication and interaction from your point of view. Say how and how often you and your friends/classmates use your cell phones, computers and social media to communicate with each other. How often do you/they use their cell phone in an actual face to face conversation? Would life change for you without this technological device? Share your results in class.

2. **Describe** how social interaction is influenced by augmented reality as presented in the text.

@ SNG-40654-005

3. **Analyse** the atmosphere of the extract by focusing on the author's choice of words.

4. **Explain** the last sentence: "You know you have free will, but don't feel like you need it".

5. Do you agree with the assumption above? **Justify** your opinion.

6. Compare your impressions of today's communication from task 1 with the author's vision. What has changed, what is still the same? Write a letter to the editor.

You're away on a business trip, attending a conference, and, wearing your Google augmented reality* glass contact lenses (because by then eyeglasses will be oh-so-last century), you step into a bar full of conventioneers*. These contacts are outfitted with both the latest speech recognition technology but they also, if need be, beam a holographic image of a keyboard, because it's easier to type certain things than speak everything.
What's more, the colors of your world through these lenses are supersaturated*. Virtual reality is, in many respects, more real, more immediate, than reality. And since people are so immersed in their Google worlds, you don't overhear conversations but rather fragments of words and ideas, often commands to the speech recognition engine* so you can operate certain functions on the device: "Video," "take a photo," "access Yelp for a nearby restaurant that serves tapas, beer, and is moderately priced," "send message," "yes," "no," "call home."
You're constantly logged into Facebook and every person you've seen on the street and in the bar is identified along with everyone in their social networks. On your left is a woman you don't know, but she's a friend of a friend of your cousin Irving's roommate's niece. Her name is Tina, a physics professor at the local university, and she likes extreme skiing, origami and baking. Tomorrow she'll be giving a presentation. You can view her slides and video now, if you'd like, and scan her bio. You don't. You think it's interesting that her favorite author is Jane Austen and thirty-seven people "liked" a post she penned* on the Heisenberg Uncertainty Principle. She's sipping what the computer deduces* to be a green apple martini and your Google-powered submicro-computer advertises a selection

**augmented reality** extended reality
**conventioneer** sb. who attends a convention/event
**saturated** *gesättigt*
**engine** computer programme
**to pen** to write
**to deduce** to conclude

of snacks to go with it, as well as a choice of vodkas and mixers, which you can order at the blink of an eye. Maybe later. [...]
CNN's news crawl keeps you up to date with the latest in current events, although you know better than to trust the most trusted name in news, and your Twitter and Facebook feeds are omnipresent. You find CNN distracting, though, so you shut it off. You decide to shoot a short video of the place and send it to friends back home who are still at work – although they are not at an office, since most people telecommute*. Your Google Contacts recommend that you approach a man standing in the corner, who works for a company you'd like to learn more about. It auto-creates a message that you approve, which takes away the awkwardness of approaching strangers in a bar. A return message pops up: He can't, but sends his virtual business card and suggests another time at the conference. You auto sync your calendars and set a date, place, and time.
Meanwhile, most everyone in the place has already sized you up, the computer tools at their disposal sifting through your social network, seeking commonalities*. You eye someone you think looks interesting but a red siren goes off. She's only 7 percent friend compatible, and data shows you will likely not have a fruitful conversation. That's okay. Messages have been streaming in, all of them auto-sent. Through this you can decide who to talk to. The biophysio meter has been gauging* the mood in the room, color coding them for convenience. Personally, you've always found that red hot conversations give you a headache while ice blue ones bore you to tears. The computer is able to pick up all the sounds in the room and sift through the conversations. You seek a color combination somewhat in the middle, a group of people not talking about sports or fashion. Oh, a group discussing politics, and when they are plotted on a graph you see they are pretty much on your end of the political spectrum.
You catch a scene at the far end of the bar. A patron* is shouting at the bartender, who refuses to serve him another drink because the glass he was holding measured his blood-alcohol level through the sweat in his fingers. He'll have to wait at least 45 minutes before he'll be permitted to order another scotch. [...]
A waiter appears, introduces himself, and leads you to the table where the people are discussing politics. Their conversation continues but your request to join the group has been granted and you take a seat. In front of you sits an apple martini with your favorite vodka – just what you ordered. The conversation is partly verbal and partially typed. Each person is able to present Wikipedia entries, news articles, video, and the like to buttress* his or her points, which are shared with other Google and Apple eyewear computing users. [...]
You command your eyewear to shut off. It asks if you are sure and you say "yes." Suddenly you are confronted with an un-Googled world. It appears drab and colorless in comparison. The music from the wall speakers sounds tinny*. The people before you are wan*, washed out, lumpy, unattractive. The art, plants, wall paint, lighting and decorations had all been shaped by your own preferences, and without the distortion field your wearable eyewear provided, the world appears as a gray, lifeless template*.
None of you last long without your Google eyewear, and accompanied by nervous laughter you switch it back on. The world you view through the prism of your computer eyewear has become your default setting.
You know you have free will, but don't feel like you need it.

Adam L. Penenberg, "The Dystopian Future of Google Glass", http://pando.com/2013/05/25/google-glass-in-10-years-the-view-from-dystopia/ 25.05.2013 [01.02.2014]

**to telecommute** to work from home using a computer

**commonalities** similarities

**to gauge** [geɪdʒ] to measure

**patron** customer

**to buttress** to support

**tinny** *blechern*

**wan** pale, dull

**template** *Vorlage, Schablone*

## Zoom in: Terminology

Augmented reality using a smart phone

**Augmented reality** (AR) is a live, direct or indirect, view of a physical, real-world environment whose elements are augmented (extended) by computer-generated sensory input such as sound, video, graphics or GPS data. It is related to a more general concept called mediated reality, in which a view of reality is modified (possibly even reduced rather than augmented) by a computer. As a result, the technology functions by enhancing one's current perception of reality. Basically, AR takes an existing picture and blends new information into it. By contrast, **virtual reality** replaces the real world with a simulated one. Augmentation is conventionally in real-time and in semantic context with environmental elements, such as sports scores on TV during a match. With the help of advanced AR technology (e.g. adding computer vision and object recognition) the information about the surrounding real world of the user becomes interactive and digitally manipulable. Artificial information about the environment and its objects can be overlaid on the real world.

# M 5 Watch Dogs: A Noir Cyberpunk Dystopia for the Era of Big Data and Cyberwarfare

Kyt Dotson

The dystopian genre is no stranger to video games. Just as novels vividly depict these dark societies, where people live in fear of an authoritarian regime, so do games. There are various examples of dystopian scenarios implemented in video games which critically extrapolate existing dangerous tendencies in society or politics.

Screenshot taken from the video game *Watch Dogs* (Watch Dogs by Ubisoft)

1. **Assess** in how far "we are all part cyborg now".
2. Does the technological "toolset" mentioned in the text improve our life or is it something to worry about? **Comment**.
3. **Evaluate** the importance of video games when it comes to raising awareness of negative tendencies in society or to criticising politics. Pay special attention to the target group of games such as *Watch Dogs*.

Video game publisher Ubisoft recently unveiled* their newest work of art *Watch Dogs* at E3 2012 and from the footage it looks like a beautiful masterpiece of contemporary-set science fiction mixed with technology people interact with every day. In it, the would-be antihero protagonist, Aiden Pierce, wanders a noir* city controlled by a master supercomputer (a "smart city" perhaps) that interconnects the entire population with cameras, cell phones, vehicle transponders, all the necessary elements of a modern-day surveillance dystopia.

The trailer is a beautiful rendering* of open-storytelling with a great deal of immersive* qualities – perhaps the best part of it is that the cyberpunk elements presented are all currently plausible: jamming the signal of all cell phones in a certain radius; using augmented reality to determine the status of a person in visual range; even causing a traffic accident by manipulating traffic lights.

The clever conceit* of the game is that all these disparate* systems are interconnected and therefore easily cross-referenced and hacked.

"*Watch Dogs* goes beyond the limits of today's open-world games by giving players the ability to control an entire city," Jonathan Morin, creative director, Ubisoft said in a statement. "In *Watch Dogs*, anything connected to the city's Central Operating System becomes a weapon. By pushing the boundaries, we can provide players with action and access to information on a scale that's never been seen in a video game before."

To those of us in the early part of the 21st century, the mobile phone is an ubiquitous* device that contains a great deal of information on us as a person. In fact, they're becoming such a central source of personal information now mobile devices are the target of hackers and malware looking for an easy payday. In the footage from the video game, the protagonist uses his iPhone-like device with augmented reality to gather information about people around him, identify affiliations, and perhaps as fluff-text*, view significant traits about them.

The premise* behind the story, and Aiden's foray* into the highly open-world of the game, is a "who watches the watchers," premise of surveillance and Big Data societies. A central computer, called the "Central Operating System" controls and tracks all the city resources; but who controls the central computer and therefore the lives of everyone in the Windy City? [...]

In a way, *Watch Dogs* feels almost like a video game about how humanity copes with technology and its inevitable corruption of the human spirit – a theme at the core of many cyberpunk works. [...]

All of these stories have been video games about how technology will affect humanity [...]. It is important to remember that we are all part cyborg now, each device that we add to our toolset increases our cyber-footprint, a cell phone, an Android tablet, a laptop. These may not be cybernetic prosthetic replacements for body parts; but they are in fact cybernetic extensions of ourselves – extra memory in the cloud on our mobile devices, a smart agent working to filter the news for us while we sleep, asynchronous communication when we're out of contact.

A game such as what Ubisoft is offering may be just the thing to entertain and amaze with just what we could do with what we have right now given the right circumstances. After all, that's what fiction does best.

Kyt Dotson, "Ubisoft's Watch Dogs: A Noir Cyberpunk Dystopia for the Era of Big Data and Cyberwarfare", http://siliconangle.com, 05.06.2012 [01.02.2014]

**to unveil** to reveal, to make known

**noir** French for dark

**rendering** visualisation

**immersive** here: deeply involving

**conceit** here: clever idea

**disparate** dissimilar, diverse

**ubiquitous** [juːˈbɪkwɪtəs] omnipresent, universal

**fluff-text** text that provides setting and context

**premise** assumption, idea

**foray** trip, journey

**ZOOM IN: Terminology**

Merging of human and machine

**Cyberpunk** is a postmodern science fiction genre expressing ideas about human nature and technology and their respective combination. It features advanced science, such as information technology and cybernetics, coupled with a degree of breakdown or radical change in the social order. Cyberpunk plots often centre on a conflict among hackers, artificial intelligences, and mega-corporations, and tend to be set in a near-future Earth. Cyberpunk writers tend to use elements from hardboiled detective fiction, film noir, and postmodernist prose to describe the often nihilistic underground side of an electronic society. In some cyberpunk writing, much of the action takes place online, in cyberspace, blurring the border between actual and virtual reality. The genre's vision of a troubled future is often called the antithesis of the generally utopian visions of the future popular in the 1940s and 1950s. William Gibson with his novel *Neuromancer* (1984) is probably the most famous writer connected with the term cyberpunk. Further famous authors are Bruce Sterling, Neil Stephenson, Pat Cadigan. The film *Blade Runner* (1982), adapted from Philip K. Dick's novel *Do Androids Dream of Electric Sheep?*, is a prominent film representation of the cyberpunk genre.

## M 6 A Declaration of the Independence of Cyberspace

### John Perry Barlow

With the Communications Decency Act of 1996 the United States Congress attempted, for the first time, to regulate pornographic material on the Internet. The CDA imposed punishment on anyone who "(A) uses an interactive computer service to send to a specific person or persons under 18 years of age, or (B) uses any interactive computer service to display in a manner available to a person under 18 years of age, any comment, request, suggestion, proposal, image, or other communication that, in context, depicts or describes, in terms patently offensive as measured by contemporary community standards, sexual or excretory activities or organs" (*Telecommunications Act,* 1996). Critics regarded this act as a violation of free speech. As a response to the Act, John Barlow wrote his "Declaration of the Independence of Cyberspace" about the legal status of the Internet.

## Zoom in: People

**John Perry Barlow** (born 1947) is an American poet, essayist and cyber rights activist. He is the former lyricist of the rock band *Grateful Dead* and current co-founder and co-chair of the Electronic Frontier Foundation (EFF). The EFF is one of the leading non-profit organisations dedicated to protecting 'digital freedom'. In 1997, John Perry Barlow was a Fellow at Harvard's Institute of Politics. He is currently a Berkman Fellow at the Harvard Law School. John Perry Barlow has written for a wide diversity of publications, ranging from *Communications of the ACM* to *The New York Times* to *Nerve*. He was on the masthead (*Titelkopf, Impressum*) of *Wired* for many years. John Perry Barlow's piece for *Wired* on the future of copyright, "The Economy of Ideas", is now taught in many law schools. His manifesto, "A Declaration of the Independence of Cyberspace", has been widely distributed on the Net and can be found on more than 20,000 sites. Partly as a consequence of the distribution of this text, John Perry Barlow was called "the Thomas Jefferson of Cyberspace" by *Yahoo Internet Life* Magazine.

1. **Outline** Barlow's arguments for rejecting governmental control of the Internet.
2. **Describe** Barlow's utopian vision of Cyberspace.
3. **Analyse** the linguistic and stylistic devices the author employs to convince the reader.
4. **Discuss** whether the Internet should be controlled by the government.

Governments of the Industrial World, you weary* giants of flesh and steel, I come from Cyberspace, the new home of Mind. On behalf of the future, I ask you of the past to leave us alone. You are not welcome among us. You have no sovereignty* where we gather.

We have no elected government, nor are we likely to have one, so I address you with no greater authority than that with which liberty itself always speaks. I declare the global social space we are building to be naturally independent of the tyrannies you seek to impose on us. You have no moral right to rule us nor do you possess any methods of enforcement we have true reason to fear.

Governments derive their just powers from the consent of the governed. You have neither solicited* nor received ours. We did not invite you. You do not know us, nor do you know our world. Cyberspace does not lie within your borders. Do not think that you can build it, as though it were a public construction project. You cannot. It is an act of nature and it grows itself through our collective actions.

You have not engaged in our great and gathering conversation, nor did you create the wealth of our marketplaces. You do not know our culture, our ethics, or the unwritten codes that already provide our society more order than could be obtained* by any of your impositions*.

You claim there are problems among us that you need to solve. You use this claim as an excuse to invade our precincts*. Many of these problems don't exist. Where there are real conflicts, where there are wrongs, we will identify them and address them by our means.

**weary** dull, tired

**sovereignty** power

**to solicit** to seek

**to obtain** to gain, to receive

**imposition** *Auferlegung*

**precinct** district, area

We are forming our own Social Contract. This governance will arise according to the conditions of our world, not yours. Our world is different.
Cyberspace consists of transactions, relationships, and thought itself, arrayed like a standing wave in the web of our communications. Ours is a world that is both everywhere and nowhere, but it is not where bodies live.
We are creating a world that all may enter without privilege or prejudice accorded by race, economic power, military force, or station of birth.
We are creating a world where anyone anywhere may express his or her beliefs, no matter how singular, without fear of being coerced* into silence or conformity.
Your legal concepts of property, expression, identity, movement, and context do not apply to us. They are all based on matter, and there is no matter here.
Our identities have no bodies, so, unlike you, we cannot obtain order by physical coercion. We believe that from ethics, enlightened self-interest, and the commonweal*, our governance will emerge. Our identities may be distributed across many of your jurisdictions. The only law that all our constituent cultures would generally recognize is the Golden Rule. We hope we will be able to build our particular solutions on that basis. But we cannot accept the solutions you are attempting to impose.
In the United States, you have today created a law, the Telecommunications Reform Act, which repudiates your own Constitution and insults the dreams of Jefferson, Washington, Mill, Madison, DeToqueville, and Brandeis. These dreams must now be born anew in us.
You are terrified of your own children, since they are natives in a world where you will always be immigrants. Because you fear them, you entrust your bureaucracies with the parental responsibilities you are too cowardly to confront yourselves. In our world, all the sentiments and expressions of humanity, from the debasing to the angelic, are parts of a seamless whole, the global conversation of bits. We cannot separate the air that chokes from the air upon which wings beat.
In China, Germany, France, Russia, Singapore, Italy and the United States, you are trying to ward off* the virus of liberty by erecting guard posts at the frontiers of Cyberspace. These may keep out the contagion* for a small time, but they will not work in a world that will soon be blanketed in bit-bearing media.
Your increasingly obsolete information industries would perpetuate* themselves by proposing laws, in America and elsewhere, that claim to own speech itself throughout the world. These laws would declare ideas to be another industrial product, no more noble than pig iron*. In our world, whatever the human mind may create can be reproduced and distributed infinitely at no cost. The global conveyance of thought no longer requires your factories to accomplish.
These increasingly hostile and colonial measures place us in the same position as those previous lovers of freedom and self-determination who had to reject the authorities of distant, uninformed powers. We must declare our virtual selves immune to your sovereignty, even as we continue to consent to your rule over our bodies. We will spread ourselves across the Planet so that no one can arrest our thoughts.
We will create a civilization of the Mind in Cyberspace. May it be more humane and fair than the world your governments have made before.

John Perry Barlow, "A Declaration of the Independence of Cyberspace", https://projects.eff.org, 08.02.1996 [01.02.2014]

**to coerce** to force

**commonweal** common welfare, public good

**to ward off** to avert, to repel
**contagion** here: the spread of an idea, the disease
**to perpetuate** to preserve

**pig iron** *Roheisen*

# M7 Cyber-Bullying, Social Media and Parental Responsibility

Sam Fiorella

In his article, published in October 2013 on huffingtonpost.com, Sam Fiorella asks for the implementation of a zero-tolerance policy on cyber-bullying. He believes that measures taken to date have only been half-hearted.

1. With reference to the picture from an anti-cyber-bullying ad on p. 74, outline the differences and similarities between cyber-bullying and 'traditional' bullying.
2. **Outline** which solutions Sam Fiorella suggests to reduce cyber-bullying.
3. **Evaluate** the author's zero-tolerance policy.
4. What would your zero-tolerance policy on cyber-bullying look like? Write a comment for an online blog concerned with bullying.
5. By referring to the cartoon, **discuss** what schools can/should and cannot do to prevent and fight cyber-bullying.

The issue of bullying has been thrust* into the national spotlight once again thanks to a rash of new teen bullying stories making the news. This despite the abundance* of celebrity public service announcements, documentaries on the subject, and the so-called "zero-tolerance" policies adopted by many school boards.

**to thrust** to throw

**abundance** wealth, large number

The sad reality is that all our efforts are being thwarted* by the growing popularity of social media, the proliferation of social networks, and the access teens have to more Internet-connected devices. The most recent story making the rounds on cable news and the Internet is Rebecca Sedwick, of Lakeland, Florida, who jumped from a cement factory tower on September 9th, 2013.

**to thwart** to block, to cross

While only two girls were arrested for bullying, which allegedly caused Sedwick to commit suicide, authorities claim that Rebecca was "terrorized" relentlessly for months by as many as 15 girls, both physically and online. One message posted to Rebecca's profile on social networks said that she should "drink bleach and die." Rebecca's mother closed her Facebook account and moved Rebecca to another school but thanks to social media, the cyber-bullying continued.

In an unrelated case, a girl with special needs in Texas is being bullied mercilessly by her classmates via text messages. Shea Shawhan, 18, a junior at Plano West Senior High School, suffers from seizures* due to a brain injury she suffered at birth. Despite her seizures, Shea participates in sports and is a member of the school's cheerleading squad. Instead of being inspired by – and celebrating the achievements of – Shea, her school mates are bullying her instead.

**seizure** *Anfall*

From one of the texts:

"Shea should just have one of her fucking seizures and die because people at West don't want her. That's the reason she has seizures, because that's karma for giving birth to a freaky slut."

Keri Riddell, Shea's mother, noticed the texts and reported the situation to the police. In addition, she accompanies her daughter during free periods at school to prevent any physical abuse from occurring. Riddell changed her daughter's cell number but the texts are still coming in to her new number.

**Social Networks and Technology Exacerbating the Issue**

For every step forward we take in raising awareness of the negative effects of bullying in our schools, bullies seem to find more channels by which to terrorize their peers and more hatred to motivate them. Can they be stopped?

In the two cases listed above, the parents of the teens being bullied took extraordinary steps such as closing a Facebook account, changing phone numbers, physically accompanying their children during school hours, and changing schools. Yet, in both cases, as with so many other similar stories across America, the bullying continued. [...]

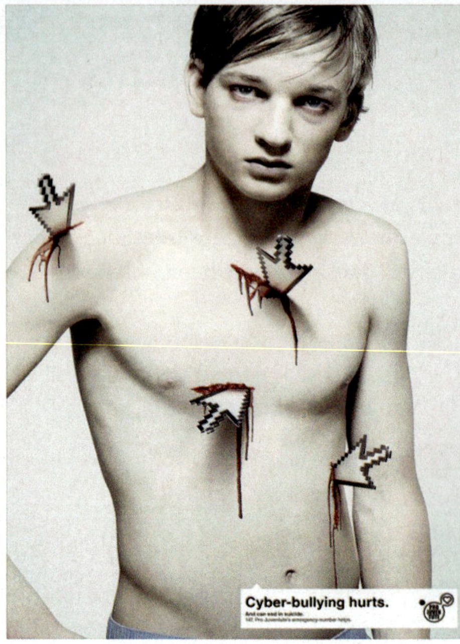

Picture for an anti-cyber-bullying campaign

**Parents' Responsibility**

In most cases of cyber-bullying, parents reject the accusations that their children could perpetrate such heinous* acts. The father of one of the girls accused of bullying Rebecca Sedwick claimed that "none of it is true ... my daughter's a good girl and I'm 100 percent sure that whatever they're saying about my daughter is not true," despite the proof the Sheriff claims to possess. While I'm happy to see that Lakeland's sheriff has charged the girls who allegedly bullied Sedwick, what consequences, if any, will their parents face? What role have the parents of bullies played in these cases? Why are parents giving young children smart phones with 24/7 access to social networks? More importantly, why are they not diligently monitoring their kids' online activity? Pre-teens typically don't have the funds or ability to purchase Internet-enabled devices or authorize Internet and mobile contracts for access to social networks. If parents are going to provide such access to their children, they must be held accountable for their online activities, including cyber-bullying. [...]

**heinous** ['heɪnəs] very wicked

**How Do We Stop Cyber-Bullying?**

We live in a politically correct world where protecting the names and privacy of students is sacred but what about the protection of kids that are being bullied? Should there not be an exception to this rule for social networks and school boards?

Why not:

- Force parents to take responsibility for the actions of their children on social networks, especially when they enable that access.
- Criminalize cyber-bullying and enforce steeper penalties for teens who bully others.
- Mandate that social networks post anti-bullying public service announcements and bullying hotline phone numbers.
- Require social networks and text-messaging services to install contextual monitoring to discover and report/block bullying comments as they happen. [...]

If we're going to have a zero-tolerance policy on this issue, then let's really have one. We can't be half-assed about it. Teens are committing suicide and we're too often left scratching our heads wondering what could have been done to prevent it.

Sam Fiorella, "Cyber-Bullying, Social Media, and Parental Responsibility", www.huffingtonpost.com, 18.10.2013 [01.02.2014]

# SPEAKING TEST

A speaking test as a substitute for a written exam will usually consist of two parts and you will probably take the test in pairs or in groups of three.

## Part I

In Part I you must show that you can speak about a text or a visual for about ten minutes. You will be given a preparation time of thirty minutes to work on three tasks. These tasks cover the same skills as in a written test, so there will be a comprehension task, an analysis task as well as an evaluation task.

| TIPS | |
|---|---|
| Make notes only. You are required to speak freely and to establish eye-contact with the interlocutors. | ✓ |
| Watch your time management. You must deal with all three tasks sufficiently in the ten minutes at your disposal. | ✓ |
| Pay attention to the task instructions. Make sure you cover all aspects of the tasks. | ✓ |
| The same rules apply as in a written test. So use your own words and neutral language only in task one, apply the TEE-technique (cf. p. 88) in task two, give a balanced assessment with reference to the text in task three. | ✓ |
| Your register must be formal. | ✓ |
| Guide your listeners through your talk. State what you are about to do and sum up your main results at the end of each task. Make use of varied sentence connectives. | ✓ |
| Speak slowly and clearly. | ✓ |

### M 8a The Circle

Dave Eggers

In Dave Eggers's novel *The Circle* (2013) a young college graduate named Mae Holland has unexpectedly landed a job at The Circle, a powerful technology company that made its fortune through TruYou, a program that removed anonymity from the Internet and allowed users to conduct all their online business using one program and one password. The Circle introduces SeeChange: a tiny, inexpensive camera capable of streaming live high-definition video which can be placed anywhere without being noticed. Soon almost the entire world can be seen online through the feed of these cameras. All for a crime-free life – at the cost of individual privacy.

1. **Outline** the reaction Mae receives after making a late night solo kayak trip.
2. **Explain** why Denise thinks that it might be a problem of low self-esteem that made Mae decide not to share her kayak experience.

**3.** The Circle's philosophical principles are "Secrets are Lies", "Sharing is Caring", "Privacy is Theft". Explain their intention. In how far is this a criticism of social media? **Comment.**

Denise put her palms on the desk, as if she might get up. "Mae, you know this is a technology company, correct?" "Of course." "And that we consider ourselves on the forefront of social media." "Yes." "And you know the term Transparency, correct?" "I do. Absolutely."

Josiah looked at Denise, hoping to calm her. She put her hands in her lap. Josiah took over. He smiled and swiped his tablet, turning a new page. "Okay. Let's go to Sunday. Tell us about Sunday."

"I just drove back." "That's it?" "I kayaked?" Josiah and Denise registered dual looks of surprise.

"You kayaked?" Josiah said. "Where?" "Just in the bay." "With who?" "No one. Just alone."

Denise and Josiah looked hurt.

"*I* kayak," Josiah said, and then typed something in his tablet, pressing very hard.

"How often do you kayak?" Denise asked Mae. "Maybe once every few weeks?"

Josiah was looking intently at his tablet. "Mae, I'm looking at your profile, I'm finding nothing about you and kayaking. No smiles, no ratings, no posts, nothing. And now you're telling me you kayak once *every few weeks*?" "Well, maybe it's less than that?" Mae laughed, but Denise and Josiah did not. Josiah continued to stare at his screen, while Denise's eyes probed* into Mae.

**to probe** to examine thoroughly

"When you go kayaking, what do you see?" "I don't know. All kinds of things." "Seals?" "Sure." "Sea lions? "Usually." "Waterbirds? Pelicans?" "Sure."

Denise tapped at her tablet. "Okay, I'm doing a search now of your name for visual documentation of any of these trips you've taken. I'm not finding anything."

"Oh, I've never brought a camera." "But how do you identify all these birds?" "I have this little guide. It's just a thing my ex-boyfriend gave me. It's a little foldable guide to local wildlife." "So it's just a pamphlet or something?" "Yeah, I mean, it's waterproof and –"

Josiah exhaled loudly. "I'm sorry," Mae said.

**tangent** here: a slightly different topic

Josiah rolled his eyes. "No, I mean, this is a tangent*, but my problem with paper is that all communication dies with it. It holds no possibility of continuity. You look at your paper brochure, and that's where it ends. It ends with *you*. Like you're the only one who matters. But think if you'd been documenting. If you'd been using a tool that would help confirm the identity of whatever birds you saw, then anyone can benefit – naturalists, students, historians, the Coast Guard. Everyone can know, then, what birds were on the bay on that day. It's just maddening, thinking of how much knowledge is lost every day through this kind of shortsightedness. And I don't want to call it selfish but –"

"No. It was. I know it was," Mae said.

Josiah softened. "But documentation aside, I'm just fascinated why you wouldn't mention anything about kayaking anywhere. I mean, it's a part of you. An *integral* part."

**scoff** an expression of doubt or mockery

Mae let out an involuntary scoff*. "I don't think it's all that integral. Or interesting, really."

Josiah looked up, his eyes fiery. "But it is!"

"Lots of people kayak," Mae said.

"That's exactly it!" Josiah said, quickly turning red. "Wouldn't you like to meet *other* people who kayak?" Josiah tapped at his screen. "There are 2,331 people near you who also like to kayak. Including *me*." [...]

Denise was looking at Mae intensely. "Mae, I have to ask a delicate question." "Okay," Mae said. "Do you think ... Well, do you think this might be an issue of self-esteem?" "Excuse me?"

"Are you reluctant to express yourself because you fear your opinions aren't valid?"

Mae had never thought about it quite this way, but it made a certain sense. Was she too shy about expressing herself? "I don't know, actually," she said.

Denise narrowed her eyes. "Mae, I'm no psychologist, but if I were, I might have a question about your sense of self-worth. We've studied some models for this kind of behavior. Not to say this kind of attitude is antisocial, but it's certainly sub-social, and certainly far from transparent. And we see that this behavior sometimes stems from a low sense of self-worth – a point of view that says, 'Oh, what I have to say isn't so important.' Do you feel that describes your point of view?"

Mae was too off-balance to see herself clearly. "Maybe," she said, buying time, knowing she shouldn't be too pliant. "But sometimes I'm sure that what I say is important. And when I have something significant to add, I definitely feel empowered to do it."

"But notice you said 'sometimes I'm sure,' " Josiah said, wagging a finger. "The 'sometimes' is interesting to me. Or concerning, I should say. Because I think you're not finding that 'sometime' frequently enough." He sat back, as if resting after the hard work of solving her was complete.

"Mae," Denise said, "we'd love if you could participate in a special program. Does that sound appealing?"

Mae knew nothing about it, but knew, because she was in trouble, and had already consumed so much of their time, she should say yes, so she smiled and said, "Absolutely."

Dave Eggers, The Circle, Alfred A. Knopf, New York 2013, p. 185–189



## Part II

Part II will usually be a collaborative task which you will work on with your partner(s) on a topic that requires you to keep up a conversation. You should also be prepared to answer questions asked by the interlocutor. Thus, the focus here clearly is on communicative competences and participating in discussions. Part II is of roughly the same length as Part I.

| TIPS | |
|---|---|
| Do not speak for too long, but give your partner a chance to contribute to the discussion. | ✓ |
| Make sure the discussion does not get stuck. You could, for example, ask for your partner's ideas or whether he/she agrees with you or not. | ✓ |
| When your partner is speaking, show that you are listening by reacting and responding appropriately. You could, for example, nod or smile as well as speak. If there is something you do not understand, ask for clarification. | ✓ |
| Watch your time management. You must deal with both tasks and you must also reach a conclusion. There will be further questions the interlocutor wants to ask you, too. | ✓ |
| Make use of varied phrases for expressing one's opinion instead of a repetitive "I think". Otherwise the same language rules apply as in Part I. | ✓ |

# M 8b Boon and Bane of Social Media

In the following you will find cartoons praising and criticising social media.

1. Take turns with your partner(s), describe the message of the cartoons and elaborate on their statements against the background of work done in class.
2. Together, come to a conclusion: Social Media – boon or bane?

# When Vision and Reality Collide

## M1 Why Dystopian Tales Like *Elysium* Often Fail

Devon Maloney

Published in August 2013 in *Wired Magazine*, a publication dedicated to the effect of technologies on culture, the economy and politics, the following article by Devon Maloney takes on one of the current dystopian action films and explains its shortcomings as a dystopian tale.

1. Recall the purpose of dystopian fiction in general.
2. Compare the medium of 'written' literature with films from the point of view of their impact on the reader/audience. Consider target audience, marketing, accessibility, convenience. Which medium is more likely to encourage people to act or to support a certain idea?

3. **Outline** the criticism of many dystopian films in general and *Elysium* in particular.
4. Create a guideline or checklist of how to write a dystopian tale. Which aspects do you have to consider?

Earth is devastated and the luxurious space station serves as an oasis for those who can afford it.

If we have anything to show for the past hundred years of world wars, space exploration, arms races, globalization and technological innovation, it's that humankind has never had better resources to identify the potential causes of its own downfall. As we become more aware of the problems we create for ourselves, fiction expressing our fears about those increasingly urgent issues has also become increasingly popular. Consider the glut* of dystopian action movies that have overloaded theaters this summer, including *Oblivion, After Earth, Pacific Rim* and most recently, *Elysium*, the sophomore* film from filmmaker and noted dystopian visionary Neil Blomkamp. [...]

[We] saw *Elysium* take issues like immigration, access to healthcare, worker's rights, and socioeconomic stratification* to their futuristic, yet logical extremes. [UCLA English professor Ursula K.] Heise notes that those extremes – the idea that the rich really could build a habitat on a space station, keeping out the poor by disenfranchising and murdering them – aren't really supposed to be taken literally*, as "apocalyptic writing is not supposed to be a forecast; it's the intensity of the apocalyptic view of the future that's the point: The darker it is, the more urgently the author calls you to reform." [...]

"With narrative films, there are two things to consider: How does it change the public debate, in policy and government, and how does it change the average moviegoer's individual perspective? The general wisdom and empirical work on that says that [the dystopian film] does raise awareness of issues, but only for a short time. Right after people have seen these movies, they're more willing to confront the problems shown in the movie, voting for politicians who promise to fight those issues, but ask them two or three months down the line, and the effect has usually worn off*." [...]

To make matters worse, Blomkamp's call for reform in *Elysium* involves an attempt to solve the complex problems he's forecasted in an extremely simplistic and nigh-magical* way – a move that goes horribly awry* and ultimately misdirects the viewer's attention *away* from the real issues at hand. Fiction and artistic license aside, Heise says in creating dystopias, the writer shoulders an implicit obligation to help people prevent the ills they perceive from worsening. In this case, that responsibility went into overdrive and combusted*.

"[*Elysium*] sets up an interesting problem, but answers it with total clichés," Heise says. "You're pointing to a big structural, socioeconomic problem, and it's going to be solved by two white guys in cyborg armor beating each other up? You've gotta be kidding ... Healthcare [and immigration were] distractions, too: The idea is raised that once everyone is a citizen and ambulances go heal everybody, the problem is solved. The problem clearly wasn't that people were sick; healthcare's inaccessibility was a symptom of a radically inequitable* economic system. These are treating the symptoms, not curing the disease."

In other words, while dystopian literature may not always change the world, it can have its uses. But the genre stops working altogether when its authors start trying to fix catastrophic, chillingly realistic problems with magical, utopian solutions. It's more likely to stick in moviegoers heads when they're left to debate the solutions on their own, as with the bleak cliffhanger ending* of Blomkamp's previous film, *District 9*.

"Excluding disaster movies, there is an imperative* in the dystopian genre, [an implied] call to action, to think about the problems before they become problems," she says. "[But] the problem with solving the problem [in the story] is that there will always be new problems coming out of your solutions," she says. "*Elysium* as a whole goes from complicated social, political and moral issues and simplifies them to black and white. I distress when movies and novels do this, because it's not as helpful as dystopias can be."

Devon Maloney, "Why Dystopian Tales Like *Elysium* Often Fail", www.wired.com, 19.08.2013 [01.02.2014]

**glut** huge amount

**sophomore** here: naive

**socioeconomic stratification** condition within a society where social classes are separated along economic lines

**literally** *buchstäblich, wörtlich*

**to wear off** to fade, to disappear

**nigh** almost

**to go awry** to go wrong

**to combust** to burn

**inequitable** unjust, unfair

**cliffhanger ending** dramatic open ending of a story

**imperative** necessity

# M2 Forget Dystopian Fiction. Sochi Is Pure Dystopian Reality

Devon Maloney

Again, Devon Maloney from *Wired Magazine* critically reflects on dystopian literature. Published in February 2014, during the Winter Olympics in Sochi, Russia, the article employs this event to focus on the inherent weaknesses of dystopian literature.

Hammer and sickle as the symbols of the former Soviet Union appeared at the Olympic opening ceremonies 2014 in Sochi, Russia, during a choreographed tour through Russian history.

1. **Describe** the criticism of the Olympics in Sochi. What does the author consider to be dystopian about them? For help, reconsider the box on p. 11.
2. **Explain** why the genre of dystopian literature is "pretty much dead" (l. 4).
3. **Examine** the strategy the author employs to convince his readers that the Olympics in Sochi are a dystopian reality. Consider rhetorical devices and line of argument.
4. **Explain** why dystopian literature has to evolve, according to the author.
5. The author claims that dystopian fiction as it is might not be useful anymore. Therefore dystopian fiction has to change. But how and to what end? Assess whether or not your guideline for writing a dystopian tale (**M 1**) fulfils this purpose.

If you're exhausted by the glut of dystopian literature that has dominated the entertainment world over the last few years, take heart: We're almost free of its chokehold*, but it's not just because the stories are all starting to look the same.
"Pretty much dead," is how one literary agent described the subgenre to the *Christian Science Monitor* back in November. It's the same line an agent gives any writer who so much

**chokehold** *Würgegriff*

**YA** young adult

**market saturation** point at which a market is no longer generating new demands for a certain product

**to ooze** to flow/leak in or out slowly
**unease** discomfort, anxiety
**eerily** creepy, spooky
**stray dogs** 'homeless' dogs
**ludicrous** ridiculous, absurd
**visceral** out of base emotional considerations

**moot** irrelevant

**NYT** The New York Times

**closed circuit** *here*: under controlled circumstances

**to be complicit** to be knowingly involved in a crime

as breathes the phrase "dystopian YA* trilogy." But while it's true that any new futuristic allegories would drown in a sea of *Hunger Games, Divergent*, and *Maze Runner* trilogies, market saturation* isn't its biggest problem. The truth is that we're realizing what those books promise; we're trading our fiction in for something bigger, scarier, and *more real*. If you want a totalitarian world that obscures its suffering and oppressed under a gleaming state-sponsored banner, look no further than the Sochi Winter Olympics – or as we might want to think of it, the Dystopian Singularity.

The two-week event, which kicked off this weekend, has oozed* unease* for months: draconian anti-gay laws that have "welcomed" participating athletes; eerily* unfinished/oddly designed/intimately surveilled hotel accommodations; government-funded, systematic "destruction" *via poison darts* of hundreds of stray dogs* (many stray in the first place due to Olympic displacement); absolutely ludicrous* amounts of alleged corruption that went into readying the city for international competition. Every headline about the Russian Games seems so incredibly, darkly fictional – even athletes' yogurt supply has come under fire! – that our bafflement finds its most visceral* outlet in trending topics.

But simple authoritarianism does not a dystopia make. As UCLA English professor Ursula K. Heise explained to WIRED back in August, most effective dystopias are slicked with a utopian glaze, a grim (if glossy) insistence that this is the paradise we've always dreamed of. Since reports began pouring in from Sochi, Russian authorities have aggressively chased criticism, attempting to redirect attentions from horror-show hotels to their glittering, multi-billion-dollar stadiums. Instead of outright gay-bashing (which, considering the relatively safe climate for homophobes in Russia, wouldn't be that absurd), Sochi mayor Anatoly Pakhomov simply claimed the conversation was moot*, because there simply weren't any gay people in his city. Besides, check out these dancing bears! And this terrifying selfie-building! And this awesome opening ceremo – oh, wait.

But here's the best-worst part: no matter how many articles use the word "dystopia," Sochi doesn't just *look* like a hellish future straight off the NYT* bestseller list. It's a complete and active masterpiece – because despite all the plot markers, despite all the freaky realities that scream *something is really wrong here*, we still tune in. Just like the *Hunger Games'* Capitol citizens, Western audiences eat up happy-faced Olympic broadcasts as readily as we have since the Games were first televised on a closed circuit* in Berlin in 1936. We'll read all the coverage as entertainment, make Twitter jokes about stray dogs, and laugh about it over drinks (even if it's to keep from crying). Six thousand athletes will compete just as they did in London in 2012, even if tourists don't quite make it out. The Olympics are the Olympics, after all. Sochi is the Dystopian Singularity because we accept it as reality – and thus are complicit* in its success. [...]

If this is really happening, though, at least we have a few protagonists. Members of the radical-feminist punk performance art collective Pussy Riot have been active, powerful critics of President Putin's regime – which is exactly how they came to the West's attention at all. After several members' arrest and political imprisonment for hooliganism (after they performed a radical protest song in Moscow's biggest cathedral), Maria "Masha" Alyokhina and Nadezhda "Nadya" Tolokonnikova were released in December just months before their two-year sentence was up. (They maintain that their release was a Putin PR stunt.) [...] Last week they appeared on *The Colbert Report* and at an Amnesty International benefit concert, where they urged people to boycott or protest the Games and the leaders overseeing them. There's no quantitative way to measure Nadya and Masha's success – and it's likely that some might miss the point – but it's a good bet that their story (and Pussy Riot's message) has resonated with audiences even if it doesn't affect their willingness to add to the ratings.

There are quieter acts of solidarity, as well, scripted straight from Katniss's victory tour*: Russian snowboarder Alexey Sobolev appeared to display a Pussy Riot member on the bottom of his board when he took to the slopes on Thursday; the same day, Google unleashed a pro-LGBT Doodle*. One could even argue that Johnny Weir's* fashion statements are marks of resistance. But these won't change the fact that things will probably worsen in Russia after the Games end and the world stops watching; the Olympics are notorious for draining economies dry and Sochi is the most expensive Games ever assembled.

Certainly, Sochi isn't single-handedly decimating the dystopia YA marketplace, but it's nonetheless a perfect example of why the genre is failing. It's not because a shallow fad has run its course; it's because the fantasies and the facts have become nearly identical. And that's the problem – Entertainment is meant to be an escape, fantasy and science-fiction in particular; movies about poverty don't do well during a recession because no one in the midst of turmoil* likes seeing their suffering splashed onto the silver screen. [...] The fact is, when the allegory starts looking like the reality, it's time for the allegory to evolve.

Devon Maloney, "Forget Dystopian Fiction. Sochi Is Pure Dystopian Reality", www.wired.com, 11.02.2014 [24.03.2014]

**Katniss's victory tour** reference to the *Hunger Games* trilogy

**LGBT** Lesbian, Gay, Bisexual and Transgender

**Doodle** here: a specially designed Google logo used on special occasions

**Johnny Weir** an American figure skater

**turmoil** chaos, confusion

**6.** Do further research on the claim that, according to the author, Sochi is an active masterpiece of a "hellish future" (l. 32). Pay special attention to the activist group Pussy Riot, their protest and the state's reaction. Give a presentation in class.

Consider the links given in the Webcode.

@ SNG-40654-006

# ZOOM IN: Words in Context

| Visions of the Future | |
|---|---|
| apocalypse [əˈpɒkəlɪps] (n.); apocalyptic (adj.) | Apokalypse; apokalyptisch |
| arms race | Wettrüsten |
| authoritarian | autoritär |
| casualty | Opfer |
| catastrophe | Katastrophe |
| chemical weapon | chemische Waffe |
| civil war | Bürgerkrieg |
| to commit crimes against humanity | Verbrechen gegen die Menschlichkeit begehen |
| to contaminate (v.); contamination (n.) | kontaminieren, verseuchen, vergiften; Kontaminierung |
| destruction (n.); destructive (adj.) | Zerstörung; zerstörerisch |
| to devastate (v.); devastation (n.) | verwüsten; Verwüstung |
| dystopia | Dystopie |
| to fall apart | auseinanderfallen |
| high-tech | hoch technologisiert |
| imaginary | imaginär, erfunden |
| irreversible | nicht mehr rückgängig zu machen |
| mankind | Menschheit |
| natural resources | Bodenschätze |
| nuclear war | Atomkrieg |
| to obliterate | auslöschen, ausmerzen |
| sophisticated | hoch entwickelt |
| utopia | Utopie |
| warfare | Kriegführung |
| weapons of mass destruction | Massenvernichtungswaffen |

| Genetic Engineering: Horror or Hope? | |
|---|---|
| to breed (v.); breeding (n.) | züchten; Züchtung |
| consumer | Verbraucher/in |
| controversial | kontrovers, umstritten |
| crop | Feldfrucht, Nutzpflanze |
| to cure (v.); cure (n) | heilen; Heilung |
| to determine sth. | etw. bestimmen |
| disease | Krankheit |
| DNA (desoxyribonucleic acid) | DNS (Desoxyribonukleinsäure) |
| ethics (n.); ethic (adj.) | Ethik; ethisch |
| extinction (n.); extinct (adj.); to become extinct (v.) | Aussterben; ausgestorben; aussterben |

| | |
|---|---|
| foetal ['fiːtl] | fötal |
| gene | Gen |
| genetics (n.); genetic (adj.) | Genetik; genetisch |
| genetic defect | genetischer Defekt |
| genetic disorder | genetische Störung |
| genetic engineering | Gentechnik |
| genetic modification (GM) | gentechnische Veränderung |
| genetic test | Gentest |
| genome | Genom |
| herbicide | Unkrautvernichtungsmittel |
| hereditary; hereditary disease | erblich, angeboren; Erbkrankheit |
| to implant sth. into sth. | etw. in etw. einpflanzen |
| infertile | unfruchtbar |
| to inherit sth. from sb. | etw. von jdm. erben |
| in vitro fertilisation | künstliche Befruchtung |
| to label sth. | etw. kennzeichnen |
| laboratory (lab) | Labor |
| mammal | Säugetier |
| morale [mɒ'rɑːl], morality (n.); moral ['mɔrəl] (adj.) | Moral; moralisch |
| mutation | Mutation |
| organ donor | Organspende |
| to patent sth. | etw. patentieren |
| patient | Patient |
| pest | Schädling |
| pesticide | Pestizid, Schädlingsbekämpfungsmittel |
| potential | Fähigkeit |
| preservation (n.); to preserve sth. | Erhaltung; etw. erhalten |
| protein | Protein, Eiweiß |
| reproductive technology | Fortpflanzungstechnologie |
| researcher; research | Forscher/in; Forschung |
| resistance to sth. | Widerstandsfähigkeit gegen etw. |
| scientist (n.); science (n.); scientific (adj.) | Naturwissenschaftler/in; Naturwissenschaft; naturwissenschaftlich |
| selective breeding | selektive Zucht |
| sexual reproduction | sexuelle Fortpflanzung |
| (embryonic) stem cell | (embryonale) Stammzelle |
| symptom | Symptom |
| test tube | Reagenzglas |
| therapeutic cloning | therapeutisches Klonen |
| toxin (n.); toxic (adj.) | Giftstoff; giftig |

| | |
|---|---|
| transgenic | transgen |
| transplantation (n.); to transplant sth. | Transplantation; etw. transplantieren/verpflanzen |
| treatment | Behandlung |
| vaccine | Impfstoff |
| yield | Ertrag |

| Tyranny of Technology? | |
|---|---|
| animate (adj.); to animate (v.) | belebt, lebendig; animieren |
| artificial intelligence (AI) | künstliche Intelligenz |
| avatar | Avatar, virtuelle Figur |
| drone | Drohne |
| to exploit (v.); exploitation (n.) | ausbeuten; Ausbeutung |
| fragmentation | Zersplitterung, Zerstückelung |
| hazard (n.); hazardous (adj.) | Gefahr; gefährlich |
| to invent (v.); invention (n.) | erfinden; Erfindung |
| microchip | Mikrochip |
| progress (n.); progressive (adj.) | Fortschritt; fortschrittlich |
| robotics | Robotertechnik |
| robot | Roboter |
| surrogate | Stellvertreter, Ersatz |
| technological advance | technologischer Fortschritt |

| Are We All Friends Now? Boon and Bane of Social Media | |
|---|---|
| application | Anwendung, Programm |
| asynchronous communication | asynchrone Kommunikation (Email, SMS, Foreneinträge, bei denen das Senden und Empfangen von Daten zeitlich versetzt abläuft) |
| augmented reality | (computergestützte) Erweiterung der Realitätswahrnehmung |
| content | Inhalt |
| cyber-footprint, digital footprint | digitale Spuren (online) |
| cyberbullying, cyber-bullying, cyber bullying | Online/Internet-Mobbing |
| default setting | Standardeinstellung |
| device | Gerät |
| engine | zentrales Kernprogramm (in der Computerprogrammierung) |
| feed | Eingabe, Einspeisung von Informationen |
| to gather information | Informationen sammeln |
| to log in/off | an-, abmelden |
| media coverage | Medienberichterstattung |
| malware | schädliches Computerprogramm |

| | |
|---|---|
| to monitor | be-/überwachen |
| persona | Rolle, Identität |
| to post | einen Beitrag verfassen |
| to register | anmelden |
| rendering | Visualisierung |
| to share | teilen, freigeben |
| to subscribe, *here: the online equivalent of signing up for a magazine (blog)* | sich anmelden, etw. abonnieren |
| surveillance | Überwachung |
| to tag (e. g. attaching a person's name to a picture) | markieren (online) |
| to transmit | übermitteln |
| tool | Hilfsprogramm, Werkzeug |
| to go viral | sich wie ein Virus verbreiten |

| **When Vision and Reality Collide** | |
|---|---|
| antagonistic | antagonistisch, gegnerisch, widerstreitend |
| to collide | kollidieren, aufeinanderprallen |
| to be mutually exclusive | sich gegenseitig ausschließen |

# Zoom in: Task instructions (*Operatoren*)

Every exam you take in English consists of three tasks referring to three different performance standards (*Anforderungsbereiche, AFB*).

## AFB I: Comprehension

**Aspects to be considered:**

- introduce your text by giving the essential information about the text at hand (author, title, text type, topic, publication, place, year, intention/target audience)
- use objective and neutral language
- use present tense and avoid contracted forms
- paraphrase (use your own words and do not use specific vocabulary which is also used in the text)
- make sure that your text is not longer than the original one
- do not state your own opinion
- do not quote

| Task instruction | Definition |
|---|---|
| describe | Give a detailed account of something. |
| outline | Give the main features, structure or general principles of a topic, omitting minor details. |
| state | Specify clearly. |
| present | (Re-)structure and write down. |
| point out | Find and explain certain aspects. |
| summarize, write a summary | Give a concise account of the main points. |

## AFB II: Analysis

**Aspects to be considered:**

- use objective and neutral language
- use present tense and avoid contracted forms
- focus only on specific parts of the text
- stick to the appropriate terminology for analysing texts (cf. skills)
- look at the structure of the text and the stylistic devices and explain the resulting function/effect (one very effective method for doing this is the TEE-method)

| T(hesis) | E(xample) | E(xplanation) |
|---|---|---|
| The author makes frequent use of alliterations/enumerations/metaphors/anaphoras/... | quote from the text | His/her intention is to emphasize/stress/underline ... |
| In addition, he/she underlines his/her point by applying numerous contrasts ... | quote from the text | These contrasts make clear that ... |

| Task instruction | Definition |
|---|---|
| analyze, examine | Describe and explain in detail certain aspects and/or features of the text. |
| characterize | Describe and examine the way in which the character(s) is/are presented. |
| examine | cf. analyze |
| explain | Describe and define in detail. |
| illustrate | Use examples to explain or make clear. |
| interpret | Make clear the meaning of something. |
| compare | Point out similarities and differences. |

## AFB III: Evaluation

In the third task, you are either supposed to evaluate the text by giving your own opinion (Evaluation), or deal with the given information in a more creative way (Re-creation of text).

**Aspects to be considered:**

- use present tense and avoid contracted forms
- prove your points with reference to the text by quoting
- clearly state your personal opinion and give reasons for it
- explicitly refer to what you have dealt with in class in regard to the topic

| Task instruction | Definition |
|---|---|
| comment | Clearly state your opinion on the topic and support your views with evidence. |
| discuss | Investigate or examine by argument; give reasons for and against. |
| justify | Show adequate grounds for decisions or conclusions. |
| contrast | Emphasize the differences between two or more things. |
| assess | Find and explain certain aspects. |

## AFB III: Evaluation: Re-creation of text

The most common assignment for task three is to transfer the information from the given text into another text type. The text type will depend on whether the original text is a fictional or non-fictional text.

**Aspects to be considered:**

- use language appropriate for the respective text type (e.g. letter to the editor: formal, conversation/dialogue: (in)formal)
- make a connection to the given text
- be aware of the formal requirements

| Task instruction | Definition |
|---|---|
| write ... | |
| – a newspaper article (report comment); | Appropriate language/register (report vs. comment)<br>Differentiation concerning<br>– facts, opinions<br>– being objective, personalization/dramatization<br>– particular case, context |
| – a speech script (talk, public/ formal speech, [debate] statement) | Appropriate language/register;<br>Introduction: address of welcome/transparency of structure;<br>Main part: structure and link to text/facts and assessment;<br>Conclusion: e.g. summary/appeal |
| – a letter/e-mail (formal letter, letter to the editor; personal letter) | Appropriate language/register; author/addressee/reason for writing/form of address/complimentary close;<br>structure: connection to topic, argumentation |
| – an interview | Appropriate language/register;<br>neutral, unbiased, unemotional interviewer;<br>introduction (topic, conversational partner);<br>structured questioning;<br>conversational partners act according to their role |
| – an interior monologue/ a conversation<br>– an alternative ending (only advanced course) | Appropriate language/register; coherence between original and continued text |

# How to Analyse Atmosphere in a Fictional Text

Atmosphere can be seen as the dominant mood or tone of a text and the feeling that is created within the story. Several factors can influence the atmosphere in a fictional text. Setting, choice of words and the characters themselves are primary means of creating atmosphere. When writing an analytical essay about the atmosphere of a fictional text it is therefore wise to combine various literary elements. At times not all elements have an equal share in influencing atmosphere, so you have to focus on one or two aspects. It consequently depends on the text at hand which elements need to be included and to what extent. The following section gives you an overview of aspects to be considered when analysing atmosphere. It provides you with a set of questions to be addressed to the text and describes some possible effects of the means the author uses.

## 1. Aspect of Analysis: Setting

In literature, the element setting is as important as characters and plot. It includes the moment in time, the geographical location as well as the scenery and moral or intellectual environment. It thereby creates the stage on which the characters act and the story takes place. The setting is considered one of the fundamental components of fiction and its interaction with the characters heavily determines the background of the atmosphere in literary texts.

| Means | Possible effect |
|---|---|
| Where does the scene or story take place geographically? Is it set outdoors or indoors? In a small chamber or large hall, open field or limited area? | • Outdoors might signify freedom of thought, action and choice.<br>• Limited areas and small areas could create the feeling of isolation and point at restricted freedom or even oppression.<br>• A creaking, old house can be scary and terrifying; a wooden house in sunlight smelling of fresh hay evokes positive feelings.<br>• The description of a place can also create a foreboding (*vorausahnende*) atmosphere of the tragic events to come (e.g. a decaying Gothic castle on a stormy night). |
| When does the story take place? Which year, season, day or time of day? | • Spring and summer usually convey optimism and positive future prospects, autumn and winter symbolise desolation and pessimism.<br>• Early morning might stand for the thirst for action; nights could create the feeling of discomfort, danger or horror.<br>• Certain time periods (e.g. 1920s) reflect specific moral attitudes, places and historical contexts. |
| What are the weather and lighting conditions like? | • Clear blue sky and sun symbolise comfort and warmth; dark, rain, fog, clouds or cold rather reveal a negative atmosphere (bleak, grim, depressive). |

| ZOOM IN: Vocabulary for Analysing the Setting in a Fictional Text | |
|---|---|
| The story/scene is set in/takes place in the year ... | *Die Geschichte/Szene spielt im Jahre ...* |
| The exterior/interior setting is ... | *Der äußere/innere Schauplatz ist ...* |
| to depict/portray | *darstellen* |
| to reflect | *widerspiegeln* |
| to create | *erschaffen* |
| to symbolise | *symbolisieren* |
| to express/verbalize | *ausdrücken* |
| to appear | *erscheinen* |
| to convey | *übermitteln* |
| to denote | *kennzeichnen* |
| display/expression of ... | *Ausdruck von ...* |
| The room/building etc. can be described as big/large/huge/ spacious/gigantic;small/narrow/tiny/cosy/constricting ... | *Der Raum/das Gebäude lässt sich beschreiben als groß/weit/ riesig/geräumig/gigantisch;klein/eng/winzig/gemütlich/ einengend ...* |
| joy, optimism, bliss, excitement, tranquility, calmness, freedom | *Freude, Optimismus, Glück, Begeisterung, Ruhe, Gelassenheit, Freiheit* |
| fear, discomfort, unrest | *Angst, Unwohlsein, Unruhe* |
| friendly, gentle, supporting, inviting, untroubled | *freundlich, sanft, unterstützend, einladend, sorglos* |
| The open range of the landscape creates a positive atmosphere mirroring the feeling of freedom. | *Durch die Weite und Offenheit der Landschaft entsteht eine positive Atmosphäre, die das Gefühl von Freiheit widerspiegelt.* |

## 2. Aspect of Analysis: Choice of Words

In literary texts, the choice of words, mainly adverbs and adjectives, can determine the atmosphere. The author will choose words according to their connotation, a meaning beyond the literal definition, that is suggested by a word in order to reveal his/her attitude towards a subject.

| Means | Possible effect |
|---|---|
| Describe the author's choice of words (nouns, verbs, adjectives or adverbs). Do they belong to a certain word field? | • Descriptive adjectives/adverbs are the key medium for creating atmosphere.<br>• They can be weak and subtle but also strong and intense.<br>• By using opposing or even contradicting adjectives, the author can create a disharmonious atmosphere and a feeling of confusion.<br>• Words which can be assorted to a certain word field underline and intensify an existing atmosphere. |
| Do the words used suggest certain connotations? | • Connotations are commonly understood cultural or emotional associations that some words carry. They are described as positive or negative depending on the word's pleasing or displeasing connection. 'Home' has mostly positive connotations (safety, family, peace). 'Politician' has mostly negative connotations: dishonest, deceptive.<br>• Connotations therefore influence the reader's feeling towards a text in a very subtle way: e. g. 'difficult' (negative) – 'challenging' (positive). |

| | |
|---|---|
| What imagery does the author use? | • Imagery is an author's use of vivid and descriptive language appealing to the human senses to deepen the reader's understanding of the work. A description of the sound of bells for example uses auditory imagery.<br>• It draws on everyday or common experience to create atmosphere. |

| ZOOM IN: Vocabulary for Analysing the Choice of Words in a Fictional Text | |
|---|---|
| By employing/using ..., the author stresses/underlines/ emphasises/puts emphasis on ... | *Indem der Autor ... benutzt/verwendet, betont er, dass ...* |
| to give/convey the impression of ... | *den Eindruck vermitteln von ...* |
| The connotation of the word ... evokes the feeling of ... | *Die Konnotation des Wortes ... erschafft ein Gefühl des/der ...* |
| By employing/using words from the semantic field of ... the author creates/establishes an atmosphere of ... | *Indem der Autor Wörter aus dem Wortfeld ... verwendet, erschafft er eine Atmosphäre von/des/der ...* |
| vivid/animated/exaggerated language | *anschauliche/lebendige/übertriebene Sprache* |
| The phrase/expression means/denotes/implies/stands for ... | *Die Phrase/der Ausdruck bedeutet/kennzeichnet/impliziert/ steht für ...* |
| The word ... suggests that/evokes associations with ... | *Das Wort ... suggeriert, dass/erweckt Assoziationen mit ...* |
| He/she predominantly employs words that are connoted positively/negatively. | *Er/sie benutzt vorwiegend positiv/negativ konnotierte Wörter.* |
| specialist terms | *Fachbegriffe* |
| tense/gloomy/insidious/cold/hopeless/nightmarish/ hostile/threatening/lonely/grim/scary/alarming | *angespannt/düster/heimtückisch/kalt/hoffnungslos/ alptraumhaft/feindlich/bedrohlich/einsam/trostlos/ beängstigend/beunruhigend* |
| light-hearted/playful/tender/liberating/warm/hopeful/ peaceful/welcoming/harmonious/vivacious/confident/ idyllic/cheerful | *heiter/verspielt/zärtlich/befreiend/warm/hoffnungsvoll/ friedlich/einladend/harmonisch/lebhaft/zuversichtlich/ idyllisch/fröhlich* |

## 3. Aspect of Analysis: Characters

| Means | Possible effect |
|---|---|
| Are the characters flat or round? | • Flat characters are minor characters, notable for a very limited range of personality traits.<br>• Round characters have complex personalities; often portrayed as conflicting and contradictory personalities. |
| Are they static or dynamic? | • In contrast to a static character, a dynamic character changes over time by for example resolving a crisis.<br>• The depth of a character or lack of it can influence the atmosphere. A round and dynamic character is more likely to create a dynamic atmosphere of change or hope than a flat character. |
| Comment on the emotional state of the character. | • Through direct or indirect characterisation, the emotional state of a character is revealed to the reader, who is usually at a certain stage of identification with this character. If a character is joyful and likeable, it will immediately influence the atmosphere (pleasant). |

| | |
|---|---|
| What is the relationship between setting and character? Does the setting influence the characters in any way? How do the characters react to the setting? | • A student sitting in his suburban home with his parents can evoke the atmosphere of safety. The same person wandering in a dark forest at night feels lost and scared, thereby changing the atmosphere.<br>• Combining a strong, malevolent (*übel wollend*) person with a place that is described in an 'evil' and threatening way amplifies a grim atmosphere.<br>• Does a place have a psychological effect on a person, thereby being the source of a certain atmosphere? |
| Would the character be/act/feel differently if the setting was different? | • This question serves as a cross-check to identify a certain relationship between setting and character and by placing a character into a different scenario the atmospheric effect can be revealed. |

## Zoom in: Vocabulary for Analysing the Characters in a Fictional Text

Characters in literary texts contribute to the creation of atmosphere no less than the setting itself. The way they are presented and act can underline or amplify a certain mood or it can modify an existing atmosphere.

| | |
|---|---|
| The protagonist is depicted/described as ... | *Der Protagonist wird dargestellt/beschrieben als ...* |
| The antagonists can be considered ... | *Der Antagonist kann als ... gesehen werden.* |
| The narrative point of view creates suspense because ... | *Die Erzählperspektive erzeugt Spannung, weil ...* |
| to emphasise/highlight/underline/accentuate | *hervorheben/unterstreichen/betonen* |
| to amplify/intensify/exaggerate | *verstärken/intensivieren/übertreiben* |
| to compare/to make a comparison between | *vergleichen* |
| to match/correspond | *entsprechen* |
| brave, shy, clever, admirable, polite, determined, gentle, generous, passionate | *mutig, schüchtern, schlau, bewundernswert, höflich, entschlossen, sanft, großzügig, leidenschaftlich* |
| cowardly, grumpy, lazy, moody, mean, selfish, deceitful, obsessive, stubborn, unpredictable | *feige, mürrisch, faul, launisch, gemein, egoistisch, hinterlistig, zwanghaft, engstirnig, unvorhersehbar* |
| The description of the dark and grim building forms a contrast to the determined and honorable character. | *Vor dem Hintergrund des als düster und bedrohlich beschriebenen Hauses stellt der resolute und ehrbare Charakter einen Kontrast dar.* |

# Acknowledgements

|action press, Hamburg: Collection Christophel 38. |Adolfsson, Mattias, Sigtuna: 50. |alamy images, Abingdon/Oxfordshire: RGB Ventures/SuperStock 33. |Artothek, Weilheim: Joseph S. Martin 54. |Cagle Cartoons, Santa Barbara, CA: © 2009 Mike Keefe 78; © 2011 Patrick Chappatte 65. |Canongate Books, Edinburgh EH1 1TE: Jane Rogers, The Testament of Jessie Lamb 14. |Cham, Jorge: www.phdcomics.com 78. |Daily Mail, London: Graphic: Wearable Gadgets In: Daily Mail online 20/07/2013 49. |ddp images GmbH, Hamburg: SIPA 70, 79. |Domke, Franz-Josef, Hannover: 20. |Fotofinder GmbH, Berlin: DNA FILMS/Kobal Collection/images.de 42; UNIVERSAL/UIP/Kobal Collection/images.de 22. |fotolia.com, New York: AlienCat 54; beermedia 79; burnhead 79; Gernot Krautberger 36; kbuntu 60; lassedesignen 6; vege 29. |Geek Culture, British Colombia: by Nitrozac & Snaggy © 2013 Geek Culture 47. |Getty Images, München: David Malan 68; New York Daily News 83; Ron Galella, Ltd. 25; YASUYOSHI CHIBA/AFP 43. |Glynn, Dylan, Toronto Ontario M4J3H9: "Utopia Dystopia", July 2010, Personal Collection © Dylan Glynn 7. |Goodreads, San Francisco, CA, United States: 10. |iStockphoto.com, Calgary: imaginima 59; Lowryn 28; sdominick 45. |Kichka, Michel: 78. |Macmillan Publishing, New York: Peter James: Perfect People, Macmillan Publishers Ltd. Copyright © Peter James, 2011 40. |Penguin Books Ltd., London: NINETEEN EIGHTY-FOUR by George Orwell (Penguin Books, 2008) Cover reproduced with permission from Penguin Books Ltd. 62; THE CHRYSALIDS by John Wyndham (Viking, 2008). Cover reproduced with permission of Penguin Books Ltd. 20. |Penguin Random House, New York: THE CIRCLE by Dave Eggers, copyright © 2013 by Dave Eggers. Used by permission of Alfred A. Knopf, an imprint of the Knopf Doubleday Publishing Group, a division of Random House LLC. All rights reserved. 76. |Picture-Alliance GmbH, Frankfurt/M.: AP Photo/Bonaventure, Lionel 81; dieKLEINERT.de/Maltz, Peter 28; dpa 34; dpa/Aleshkovsky, Mitya 83; dpa/Pain, Andre 63; dpa/Spata, Ole 66; dpa/Thissen, Bernd 13; epa/Press Association 28 u.r.; Haas, Jan 71; Mary Evans Picture Library 55, 56. |REUTERS, Berlin: Mario Anzuoni 31; Steve Crisp 64. |Scholastic Inc., New York: From THE HUNGER GAMES by Suzanne Collins. Scholastic Inc./Scholastic Press, cover illustration by Tim O'Brien. Used by permission. 18. |Shutterstock.com, New York: sam 72 44. |Stiftung Pro Juventute, Zürich: 74. |The Garage, Amsterdam: courtesy the artists Laser 31.4 8. |toonpool.com, Berlin, Castrop-Rauxel: Lynch 78. |Ubisoft GmbH, Düsseldorf: Watch Dogs by Ubisoft 68. |ullstein bild, Berlin: 62. |vario images, Bonn: 28. |Walker Books Ltd., London: Copyright © 2002 M.T. Anderson, FEED by M.T. Anderson, Reproduced by permission of Walker Books Ltd, London SE11 5HJ www.walker.co.uk 16. |Wilcox, Cathy: 73.